ANALYZING THE ISSUES

CRITICAL PERSPECTIVES ON
THE MINIMUM WAGE

Edited by Anne C. Cunningham

Published in 2017 by Enslow Publishing, LLC
101 W. 23rd Street, Suite 240, New York, NY 10011

Library of Congress Cataloging-in-Publication Data

Names: Cunningham, Anne C., editor.
Title: Critical perspectives on the minimum wage / edited by Anne C.
Cunningham.
Description: New York, NY : Enslow Publishing, 2017. | Series: Analyzing
the issues | Includes bibliographical references and index.
Identifiers: LCCN 2015050615 | ISBN 9780766076754 (library bound)
Subjects: LCSH: Minimum wage—United States—Juvenile literature. |
Minimum wage—Law and legislation—United States—Juvenile literature.
Classification: LCC HD4918 .C75 2017 | DDC 331.2/30973—dc23
LC record available at http://lccn.loc.gov/2015050615

Printed in the United States of America

To Our Readers: We have done our best to make sure all website addresses
in this book were active and appropriate when we went to press. However,
the author and the publisher have no control over and assume no
liability for the material available on those websites or on any websites
they may link to. Any comments or suggestions can be sent by e-mail to
customerservice@enslow.com.

Excerpts and articles have been reproduced with the permission of the
copyright holders.

Photo Credits: Cover, Anadolu Agency/Anadolu Agency Collection/Getty
Images (rally for higher wages), Thaiview/Shutterstock.com (background,
pp. 4–5 background), gbreezy/Shutterstock.com (magnifying glass on spine);
p. 4 Ghornstern/Shutterstock.com (header design element, chapter start
background throughout book.

CONTENTS

INTRODUCTION

In our historical moment, corporate and stock market profits are at a record high. Yet the chasm separating the majority of working Americans from the wealthiest in our society is wider than any time since 1929, prior to the Great Depression. If economic recovery has indeed followed the 2008 financial collapse, the majority of the population is certainly not enjoying the fruits of this recovery.

However, there are signs that more and more people view this state of affairs as unacceptable, and are endeavoring to change it. Led by groups such as "Fight for $15," a reinvigorated labor movement is addressing structural inequality with a mix of traditional union organizing and novel tactics. One of their successful plays has been to focus on raising wages for minimum wage workers in highly profitable industries such as fast food. In doing so, activists have transformed the minimum wage into a wedge issue towards the larger goal of reducing inequality across the socio-economic spectrum. Will this strategy be effective? How much pushback can we expect? Finally, will struggling middle-class Americans also reap benefits? As we'll see, the effort to raise the minimum wage is also a means to address pernicious income inequality— and to strategize solutions to this growing problem.

Owing to this context, discourse about the minimum wage is typically infused with unusually strong moral rhetoric. This renders "pure" economic analysis difficult—though perhaps justifiably so. The field of economics is not neutral. Rather, it arose coextensively with industrial capitalism, and its prescriptions historically benefit the business class above other social classes. The study of the minimum wage as a quasi-objective, isolated economic phenomenon has practical limitations due to ingrained institutional bias. Nonetheless, it is useful to understand the economic principles underlying wages. After all, these terms frame the parameters of political discussion, legal challenges, and media coverage.

According to classical economics, wages are a key variable influencing the supply and demand curves that regulate labor markets. As the economists surveyed in Chapter One attest, when wages go up, we can expect negative consequences. Employers unwilling to absorb increased labor costs will fire workers, cut back hours, and automate or outsource jobs. This causes the unemployment rate to rise. In addition, prices may go up, which can lead to inflation and slower job growth. For these reasons, many economists caution against raising minimum wages. They claim it will hurt the least-skilled workers most, since employers will fire those whose wage is higher than the marginal dollar value of their productivity. To the chagrin of these economists, most Americans are unconvinced by the "wage/job tradeoff" argument, believing that poverty-level wages are simply unfair. Economists in turn dismiss this position as well intentioned, but naïve and uniformed. So who is right?

The federal minimum wage is currently $7.25 per hour, well below living wage standards. That is to say, a full-time worker earning minimum wage cannot support the basic necessities of life without assistance of some form. There is ample evidence to support this. According to the UC Berkeley Labor Center, low wages cost upwards of 150 billion dollars each year, since programs for low-income workers such as SNAP (commonly known as food stamps) and Medicaid are subsidized by taxpayers. Some states and municipalities have responded by passing laws or ballot initiatives raising the minimum wage locally. However, since these are often relatively expensive cities such as San Francisco, New York, Seattle, and Los Angeles, the purchasing power of higher wages is arguably negated by high rents and associated costs of living.

Accounts of the working poor, single parents juggling multiple jobs, and millennials unable to afford living independently from their families are quite common. These testimonials rankle a core American belief that full-time work should afford financial independence and economic advancement. This narrative certainly has tremendous staying power, but has only been a practical reality during the post-World War Two economic boom. Moreover, voters oppose overtly redistributive economic policies, despite supporting a living wage in theory. However, signs such as Bernie Sanders' popular presidential campaign focusing on inequality show that this ideology, too, can change.

As many of the articles included in this volume make clear, it's easy to oppose rampant and growing economic inequality, but predicting the extent to which a minimum wage increase will rectify this imbalance is much more difficult. The aim of this collection is to guide readers through this debate, trace its history, and situate the minimum wage as one important component of the broader struggle to secure basic economic rights for all.

CHAPTER 1

WHAT THE EXPERTS SAY

In 1938, Franklin Roosevelt passed the Fair Labor Standards Act. Among other important labor reforms and protections, the FLSA enacted a nationwide minimum wage for the first time—then set at twenty-five cents per hour. While the aim of minimum wage legislation was to protect workers from exploitation and reduce poverty, economists and policy experts are divided on the extent to which wage laws have been effective in achieving these ends, especially in regard to the latter goal.

Notable researchers in the field such as David Neumark and William L. Wascher argue that despite "right and proper" intentions, evidence that raising the minimum wage lifts workers out of poverty is dubious at best. In the introductory chapter to their influential 2009 book, *Minimum Wages*, which is reprinted below, the economists conclude that minimum wage hikes reduce employment and income, particularly among the least-skilled workers. Moreover, they found no solid evidence that increasing the minimum wage reduces poverty. Their study cautions against policy initiatives aimed at raising the minimum wage, although the authors do concede to some ambiguity in their findings.

The second and third articles examined in this chapter also emphasize the negative trade-offs of higher minimum wages such as increased aggregate unemployment and possible inflation due to compensatory price increases. Pierre Lemieux notes that taking a position on this trade-off brings "extra-economic value judgments" into play, yet also upholds a categorical distinction between economists, who tend to caution against wage increases, and non-specialists, who tend to favor them. Presumably, in this view the economist's role is to protect ordinary people from their own ignorance and resulting poor decisions. Yet if one's position on wages involves "extra-economic" valuation, minimum wage policy becomes as much a philosophical, political, and class issue as an economic one. This should cause us to view the recommendations of professional economists with a critical eye.

The chapter closes with a summary of the pros and cons of an increased minimum wage, and includes demographic information concerning who earns minimum wage, inviting readers to draw their own conclusions. Which side do you come down on?

There is ample evidence to suggest that increasing the minimum wage is not necessarily the best solution to inequality. Nonetheless, complete data on the subject is difficult to accurately interpret, and often fails to take every variable into account. Regardless of the political expediency of specific wage laws and ballot initiatives, we can expect the debate among experts and economists over minimum wage policy to continue into the foreseeable future.

EXCERPT FROM THE INTRODUCTION TO *MINIMUM WAGES*, BY DAVID NEUMARK AND WILLIAM L. WASCHER, MASSACHUSETTS INSTITUTE OF TECHNOLOGY, 2008, BY THE PERMISSION OF THE MIT PRESS

1.1 THE MINIMUM WAGE CONTROVERSY

The minimum wage has been a core element of public policy for more than a century. Originating in the 1890s in New Zealand and Australia, minimum wages spread to the United Kingdom in 1909 and to nearly one-third of U.S. states during the next two decades. In 1938, the U.S. Congress passed a federal minimum wage law as part of the Fair Labor Standards Act. Since that time, minimum wages have been introduced in some form or another in numerous other industrialized countries, as well as in some developing countries. As a result, by the 1990s, minimum wages existed in well over one hundred countries from all parts of the world, and the International Labour Organization (ILO) has designated the minimum wage as an international labor standard (International Labour Organization 2006).

Minimum wages were originally proposed as a means to combat the proliferation of so-called sweatshops in manufacturing industries. These sweatshops employed considerable numbers of women and youths and paid them what were generally regarded as substandard wages. In particular, employers were viewed as having disproportionate bargaining power over such workers, and the minimum wage was intended to ensure that they received a "fair" wage for their work. Over time, however, proponents of minimum wages increasingly advocated them as a way to help individuals or families achieve self-sufficiency, and, as a result, coverage of minimum wage laws was extended to men and to workers in most low-paid occupations.

The goals associated with the minimum wage are widely accepted as right and proper. However, there is much less agreement about whether the minimum wage is effective at attaining these goals. Although overwhelmingly popular with the public in the United States, the minimum wage has, from the time of its introduction, been highly controversial in the political arena. In addition, minimum wages have typically received less support from economists, who from the very beginning of the minimum wage debate pointed to the potential loss of jobs stemming from a wage floor. Despite decades of economic research, policy debates about the costs and benefits of minimum wages continue to the present day.

1.2 OUR RESEARCH ON MINIMUM WAGES

Research on the economic effects of the minimum wage had largely come to a halt in the 1980s, following the publication of the extensive report of the Minimum Wage Study Commission (1981). This landmark report included studies by a virtual "Who's Who?" of labor economists working in the United States at that time. During that decade, when we were completing our graduate education, the common advice we received was to find some other topic to research, as it seemed that virtually everything there was to be known about minimum wages was covered in the commission's report or in other research published prior to the report.

However, in our jobs at the Federal Reserve Board in the late 1980s, where we followed labor market developments particularly closely, we were struck by the increasing number of state legislatures that were setting minimum wages above the federal level. (1) In particular, we saw this state-level variation in minimum wages as an opportunity to improve upon the earlier evidence on how minimum wages affected employment. That earlier evidence was largely based on aggregate time-series data, which posed difficulties for reliably estimating the employment effects of minimum wages because of the limited variation in the federal minimum wage and the absence of valid counterfactual information on what would have happened to the economy in the absence of higher minimum wages. Taking advantage of this opportunity, in our first study of the employment effects of the minimum wage, we constructed a cross-section time-series panel of state minimum wages and labor market conditions, which effectively used states without a minimum wage increase as a comparison group for states that raised their minimum wage.

Not surprisingly, perhaps, we were not the only economists who had this idea, and an early set of papers published in a symposium in the *Industrial and Labor Relations Review* (ILRR) kick-started a new wave of research into the employment effects of minimum wages. This wave of research, which is often referred to as the "new minimum wage research," has continued unabated, with well over one hundred papers on this topic published since then, both for the United States— where state minimum wage variation has remained a prominent feature of the policy landscape—and for other industrialized and developing countries.

In the mid-1990s, we began to branch out from our original focus on the employment effects of minimum wages to consider their other consequences. This broadening of our research was prompted by our view that evidence on the employment effects of minimum wages is, taken alone, insufficient to inform the policy debate over the effects of minimum wages. In particular, even if minimum wages result in lower employment for low-skilled groups, there may be other benefits of minimum wages that trade off favorably against the disemployment effects, as well as other costs.

This inquiry led us in two directions. First, given the evidence that minimum wages play an important role in youth labor markets, it seemed natural to ask what other consequences they might have for youths. For example, if minimum wages reduce employment, do they also encourage young people to stay in school because of the decrease in job opportunities or to acquire more skills to raise their productivity to a level at which they would not be priced out of the labor market by a minimum wage? Conversely, does a higher minimum wage induce some teenagers or young adults to leave school in the hope of landing a job paying a higher wage because of the higher minimum? Similarly, do minimum wages deter firms from providing training to young workers, hence curtailing an important source of future wage growth? And finally, what are the longer-run effects of the minimum wage on the acquisition of skills? These questions had received some attention in earlier research, but as in the case of employment effects, the emergence of the greater variation in minimum wages across states in the late 1980s provided an opportunity to obtain new—and arguably superior—evidence on the effects of minimum wages.

The second direction our research took is one that we regard as especially important from a policy perspective. In particular, we see the principal intent of the minimum wage as helping to raise incomes of low-income families. This implies that the principal criterion for decisions about raising the minimum wage is whether doing so has beneficial effects for the distribution of family incomes—reducing poverty or increasing incomes at the bottom of the distribution. Again, this question had been considered in research predating the new minimum wage research, but the available evidence was limited and ambiguous.

1.3 PLAN OF THE BOOK

This book describes the findings of nearly two decades of research on minimum wages. It synthesizes and presents the evidence we have accumulated across nearly thirty research papers and provides a comprehensive discussion of other research that touches on the same questions we have considered, as well as on other topics central to the debate over minimum wages. In much of the book, we emphasize evidence for the United States. However, where possible, we also discuss research for other industrialized and developing countries.

We begin in chapter 2 with a brief history of the minimum wage. Although we touch briefly on its genesis in Australia and New Zealand in the late 1800s, our discussion focuses mostly on the development and evolution of minimum wage policies in the United States, and on the legal and political challenges that accompanied the efforts to enact these policies. In addition, this chapter summarizes the early debate and research among economists regarding the effects of minimum wages, a debate that to a remarkable degree foreshadowed the issues and questions raised in contemporary research.

Chapter 3 focuses on the issue that has dominated research and debate on the minimum wage—its effects on employment. After a brief discussion of the theory of the minimum wage and employment, we summarize the extensive body of contemporary research launched by the 1992 *ILRR* symposium. This literature is so extensive that we limit our discussion to our own research and to what we view as the most important or compelling evidence from the larger body of research. (2)

In chapter 4, we turn to the distributional effects of minimum wages, focusing first on the relationship between minimum wages and the distribution of individual wages. The substantial increase in wage inequality in the United States in recent decades has brought this issue to the forefront, with researchers asking whether minimum wage policies—in particular, the general stagnation of the federal minimum wage—have contributed to the rise in inequality. In addition, research on the effects of minimum wages on the wage distribution contributes to our understanding of how minimum wages affect the labor market, and is a precursor to considering the effects of minimum wages on the distribution of family incomes.

Chapter 5 examines the effects of the minimum wage on the distribution of family incomes. We first consider the relationship between low-wage workers and low-income families. Although it has long been recognized that the two are not synonymous, we discuss updated evidence on the extent to which minimum-wage workers are concentrated in low-income families. We then turn to evidence that parallels much of the minimum wage employment literature in terms of empirical methods, but focuses instead on how minimum wages affect family incomes. This analysis considers—although is not limited to—the question of whether higher minimum wages reduce poverty.

The possible effects of minimum wages on schooling and training, and other potential effects of minimum wages on the acquisition of skills, are the topic of chapter 6. We begin by studying the direct effects of minimum wages on schooling, focusing both on their overall effects and on differences in the effects of minimum wages across skill groups. For example, we ask whether minimum wage increases disproportionately reduce employment opportunities for teenagers who have already dropped out of school, and whether higher-skill workers who may be enticed to leave school by a higher minimum wage displace high school dropouts from the labor market. We then turn to the effects of minimum wages on training, a topic that is relevant to individuals whose employment status is not influenced by the minimum wage, but whose terms of employment may be affected. Because the effects of minimum wages on both training and schooling (as well as foregone labor market experience stemming from reduced employment opportunities) may have longer-lasting consequences, we also present evidence on the longer-run effects of minimum wages on workers' wages and earnings even after their wages have risen above the minimum wage.

Our work—and indeed of most of the research on the minimum wage—emphasizes the effects of minimum wages on individual workers and families. But the broader economic effects of minimum wages on profits, prices, and inflation have also been the subject of some research, and chapter 7 discusses this evidence.

In chapter 8, we turn from studying questions about *how* minimum wages affect workers and the economy to questions about the political economy of minimum wages. That is, rather than viewing minimum wages as mandated wage floors that fall from the sky, we examine the factors that influence the decisions of politicians (and others) to support or oppose higher minimum wages. As part of this inquiry, we also consider why minimum wages remain so popular even though many economists oppose them (although they certainly do not oppose them unanimously). Finally, we also discuss the newest manifestation of mandated wage floors—"living wages," which are enacted at the city level and cover a narrower set of workers. After a brief overview of evidence on the effects of living wages, we consider similar political economy questions, asking why living wage laws have arisen and why they take on particular forms.

Finally, in chapter 9, we provide a summary of our evidence, offer some concluding thoughts, and discuss implications for public policy.

1.4 OUR APPROACH AND KEY CONCLUSIONS

As we emphasize throughout this book, we believe that questions about the economic effects of the minimum wage need to be resolved empirically. Economic theory is valuable in suggesting testable hypotheses about the potential influences of minimum wages, and in that sense, it helps guide the empirical analysis. But economic theory rarely makes firm predictions about the effects of minimum wages on the outcomes we consider, and in many cases makes no prediction at all. And, even when the theoretical predictions are unambiguous, they rarely tell us about the magnitude of the effect. As a result, in this book we emphasize what the data have to say about various effects of minimum wages, and the corresponding implications both for public policy and for our understanding of how labor markets work.

Based on the extensive research we have done, and our reading of the research done by others, we arrive at the following four main conclusions regarding the outcomes that are central to policy debate about minimum wages. First, minimum wages reduce employment opportunities for less-skilled workers, especially those who are most directly affected by the minimum wage. Second, although minimum wages compress the wage distribution, because of employment and hours declines among those whose wages are most affected by minimum wage increases, a higher minimum wage tends to reduce rather than to increase the earnings of the lowest-skilled individuals. Third, minimum wages do not, on net, reduce poverty or otherwise help low-income families, but primarily redistribute income among low-income families and may increase poverty. Fourth, minimum wages appear to have adverse longer-run effects on wages and earnings, in part because they hinder the acquisition of human capital. The latter two sets of conclusions, relating to the effects of minimum wages on the income distribution and on skills, come largely from U.S. evidence; correspondingly, our conclusions apply most strongly to the evaluation of minimum wage policies in the United States.

We state these conclusions bluntly here because we believe they are justified based on the evidence. Nonetheless, as will become clear during the reading of this book, research on the many facets of minimum wages is characterized by continuing disagreement and controversy. As a result, we are under no illusion that all readers of this book will agree fully with our conclusions. However, regardless of whether the reader is convinced by our analysis, we hope that our book will be viewed as providing a thorough and dispassionate study of what has become a remarkably extensive body of research.

1. Are there any areas of this study you disagree with? For example, how might the authors' analysis of youth employment trends be incomplete?

2. Taking the argument that raising the minimum wage hurts least-skilled workers most, why don't these workers typically oppose such measures?

"FROM MINIMUM WAGES TO MAXIMUM POLITICS: WHY IS THERE SUCH A DIFFERENCE OF OPINION ON THE EMPLOYMENT EFFECTS OF A MINIMUM WAGE INCREASE?" BY PIERRE LEMIEUX, FROM *REGULATION*, SUMMER 2014

In a report issued last February, the Congressional Budget Office (CBO) estimated that raising the federal minimum wage from $7.25 to $10.10 an hour--a 39 percent increase advocated by President Obama--would reduce U.S. employment by hundreds of thousands of jobs. Just a few weeks earlier, more than 600 economists joined seven economics Nobel laureates in endorsing the proposal and claiming that it would have "little or no negative effect on employment." Then, in March, a statement signed by more than 500 economists, including three Nobel laureates, asked the federal government to think twice before increasing the minimum wage. (Disclosure: I was among the signatories of that statement.) Which group of economists is correct, and why is there such a difference of opinion?

The CBO—a nonpartisan, credible research bureau of the U.S. Congress--offers a best-estimate that increasing the federal minimum wage to $10.10 in three annual steps would, by the second half of 2016, deprive 500,000 workers of their jobs. The range of the estimate extends from a very light decrease in employment to one million workers out of work. Those workers would, of course, be made much poorer, but the tradeoff for their losses would be higher compensation for as many as 33 million other workers who would keep their jobs. The CBO estimates that similar, but smaller, effects would follow an increase of the minimum wage to $9 over two years.

The CBO report is quite prudent, incorporating all factors that could benefit employment and incomes. For example, it includes an increase of "a few tens of thousands of workers" (in the $ 10.10 scenario) whose jobs would be created by a Keynesian boost of aggregate demand caused by the higher minimum wage. It recognizes that its estimates are full of uncertainties, as illustrated by its assessment of a one-third chance that the employment effect will be out of the forecasted range. Nonetheless, the CBO concludes that the proposed increases in the minimum wage would likely create unemployment.

THE WEIGHT OF THE EVIDENCE

This conclusion is not surprising. There is no good theoretical reason why a minimum wage, if it is binding on some employers, would have anything but a negative effect on employment. If the labor market is competitive (which it certainly is, especially at the bottom of the employment ladder), then any employer will let go--or not hire--an employee whose marginal productivity is lower than the minimum wage (plus payroll taxes and other employment costs) that the employer is obliged to pay.

A large number of empirical studies have confirmed that a minimum wage, if set above the equilibrium wage level, will destroy jobs. In their seminal 2008 book *Minimum Wages*, David Neumark and William Wascher present a review of empirical research on minimum wages in the United States. They conclude that there is plenty of evidence that "minimum wages reduce employment opportunities for less-skilled workers," and they admit that their own research changed their prior views on the weight of evidence regarding the effects of minimum wages.

Anecdotal evidence that raising the minimum wage hurts employment is not hard to find. Last year, the left-wing magazine *The Nation* started an online petition demanding that Walmart boost its workers' average hourly wage from $8.18 an hour to $12. Walmart countered that *The Nation* had only recently increased its intern stipends to the equivalent of the federal minimum wage of $7.25 (previously taking advantage of an exception that young people who are hired for less than 90 days need only be paid $4.25 an hour). The magazine conceded, "We are not yet certain how this will work out long term, but for the fall we are anticipating hiring 10 interns rather than 12."

Yet, some recent empirical research (summarized by John Schmitt in a 2013 paper for the Center for Economic and Policy Research) finds little or no negative employment effect from increasing the minimum wage. In a forthcoming article, Neumark, J. M. Ian Salas, and Wascher criticize the econometric methods used in that research. The academic debate seems to be turning into arcane econometric disagreements. The more arcane the debate, the less we should be swayed from standard economic theory, according to which the demand curve for labor (like all demand curves) has a negative slope. Perhaps the negative employment effect of minimum wages is smaller than was previously thought, but it is hard to deny that there is an effect.

Even Paul Krugman is prudent in his evaluation of the evidence, affixing some telling qualifiers to his bold policy recommendations. An increase in the minimum wage, he wrote in a 2013 *New York Times* column, "would have *overwhelmingly positive* effects; it would have "*little* if any negative effect ... on unemployment"; "*modest* increases ... *don't necessarily* reduce the number of jobs"; and "the *main effect* of a rise in minimum wages is a rise in the incomes of hard-working but low-paid Americans" (my emphasis). Those qualifiers seem to imply that even Krugman recognizes that some effects will be negative and that even a modest increase (let alone a 39 percent increase) in the minimum wage may reduce the number of jobs, and perhaps that *secondary effects* would reduce the incomes of *some* hard-working but low-paid Americans.

Yet, Krugman concludes (speaking about Republican leaders opposed to raising the minimum wage), that "[t]hey say that they're concerned about the people who might lose their jobs, never mind the evidence that this won't actually happen." So "we should raise the minimum wage, now." Why so much certainty in the policy prescription advanced by Krugman and economists of his obedience?

HOW CAN ECONOMISTS BE WRONG?

Among the general public, opinion surveys show a massive support--around 75 percent--for increasing the minimum wage. This stance among people with no economic background is not surprising. Only a small minority is hurt by minimum wages. Around 5 percent of employed workers receive the current minimum wage or (given various legal exceptions) less. (The proportion would be a bit higher if we consider state laws; as of the beginning of this year, 21 states had a higher minimum wage than the federal wage.) The half-million workers that the CBO estimates would lose their jobs if the federal minimum wage were raised to $10.10 an hour represent only one-third of 1 percent of the employed work force. Moreover, as generally is the case in politics, voters remain rationally ignorant of the issue and the relevant research.

On minimum wages (like on many other issues), economists take a different stance than the general public, although economists are not as free-market as many people assume. Most surveys suggest that American economists are less favorably disposed to the minimum wage than the general public. They are split about half and half on its desirability, having perhaps become more supportive than they used to be.

To explain why so many economists support the minimum wage, Neumark and Wascher suggest that the average economist is simply not familiar with research in a field different from his primary specialization. There might be something to this explanation, but one wonders why, before going public, economists would not bother to review the literature.

In late 2006, Daniel Klein and Stewart Dompe surveyed a group of economists who had signed a public statement endorsing a minimum wage increase. They found that roughly two-thirds of the respondents conceded that raising the minimum wage would have some disemployment effects (though most of them characterized the effects as "minor"). Among other questions, Klein and Dompe asked the respondents if they believed minimum wages to be coercive and thus contrary to liberty. About three-fourths did not believe so. Although coercion is a more complex notion than many think, some write-in comments (which respondents were encouraged to add) seem remarkably naive--like, for example, these two from two different respondents:

> "I do not subscribe to this definition of liberty. For me, it has more to do with free speech and freedom of association and other civil liberties."

> "[To me, the primary meaning of liberty is] Freedom of expression."

In other words, those respondents seem to believe that liberty is only important if it involves a field of activity they personally value.

Is this naiveté or something else? That question leads us to another reason why some economists favor minimum wages: they may simply espouse values about distribution that are different from those of economists on the other side of the issue. Economists promoting minimum wages may be willing to make a different tradeoff between winners and losers, between those who lose their jobs and those who stay employed at higher wages. From the Klein and Dompe survey, we can conclude that two-thirds of respondents were conscious of a tradeoff against the unemployed, and were willing to make it. They prefer that some people lose their jobs in order that others benefit from redistribution (mainly from business owners, according to many respondents). This sort of value-laden distributive judgment is the essence of politics.

Another reason why many economists have abandoned their skepticism toward the minimum wage may simply be that they follow their fans--that is, they feel obliged to satisfy their fans' expectations. Like other intellectuals, economists are not only influenced by their political or academic bosses, they are also subject to what their admirers expect from them. This dynamic may have a stronger effect on more famous economists for the simple reasons that they have more fans. Krugman's views, for example, have become less scholarly as he's become more popular and politically active.

All this does not bode well for the credibility of economics as a science. When acting as a policy adviser, the economist cannot avoid having skin in the game--contrary to the physicist, whose deep personal values are probably not challenged much by the fate of Shrodinger's cat, whether dead or alive or both. That most economists know little about welfare economics does not help them distinguish between positive analysis and value judgments.

A PROBLEM IN WELFARE ECONOMICS

However you interpret the data, a minimum wage increase will harm some people and benefit others. It is inconceivable that such a policy would benefit everyone and harm no one. That leaves us with the standard problem in welfare economics: how to evaluate a policy measure that is not a Pareto improvement. Such an evaluation cannot be done without making extra-economic value judgments.

Imagine a situation where, before establishing a minimum wage, 5 percent of employed workers earned a wage lower than the proposed minimum. Many of those low-wage people would be poor, although virtually all who wanted a job could get one. A certain distribution of income (and utility) would thereby be generated. At the bottom of the distribution, poverty would be a consequence of everybody's liberty to enter into employment contracts at mutually agreed upon wages.

Under a minimum wage law or an increase in that wage, the distribution of income (and utility) is changed. Some of the poor, as well as some of the non-poor, get higher wages. But it is very likely that others will lose their jobs and become poorer. Whether the new poor number one million, 500,000 or just one, the welfare economics problem is the same. The distribution has been changed by coercive government regulation, "coercive" meaning that the new poor would not comply with the law if they, and their potential employers, were not forced to do so. At the bottom of the distribution, some poverty results from political diktats and bureaucratic enforcement or, in other terms, from the coercive power of some individuals over others.

Answering the liberty-coercion question in the Klein and Dompe survey, one economist commented: "Have you ever had to sit and listen to children crying for want of food?" That comment is the stuff of public relations dreams, but it also illustrates our welfare problem. Let's pursue the story in those terms.

Suppose that, in contemporary America, some children cry because they are hungry. They are probably few in number, but even if there is just one single hungry child, our welfare calculation must count him. (Note in passing how strange such a situation is when all levels of U.S. government devote 40 percent of their expenditures, or around 15 percent of gross national product, to social transfers and social programs. Perhaps the state is not that great after all.)

If the CBO's estimates are correct, there probably will be fewer crying children after the minimum wage has been increased to $10.10 because the measure will have pulled 900,000 individuals above the official poverty level. Those individuals include children in poor families, but they are not net crying children. Some previously crying children will be fed, and stop crying; but other children, in families with one or more of the 500,000 new unemployed, will lose their food and start crying or cry all the harder.

The plights of those two groups of children (and their parents) have very different sources. The ones crying before the increase in the minimum wage owed their impoverished condition to the impersonal result of everybody's equal liberty. The plight of the new crying babes, after the minimum wage enactment or increase, will have been directly caused by the people holding political power.

Some economists argue that there will be little or no dis-employment effect because of efficiency gains--in other words, employers will make their employees work harder in order to justify the higher wages. The question is, why didn't the employers achieve those gains before a new minimum wage was imposed? Perhaps those employers weren't actively trying to maximize profits until the politicians changed the minimum wage--but that seems unlikely. The more likely reason is that it was not profitable for the employers to do so, perhaps because the low-productivity employees did not want to--or could not--work harder. If, after a minimum wage is imposed, employers find ways to work their employees harder instead of firing them, then you may have fewer crying babies, but you will also have some crying, exploited workers. There is no such thing as a free lunch.

Feeding crying children, even if there is only a small number of them, is a worthy objective. But trying to achieve it through political coercion not only implies making tradeoffs among individuals, but it also increases the burden of regulation and dampens economic growth and prosperity. Econometric estimates by John Dawson and John Seater suggest that if federal regulation had remained at its 1949 level, the average American would now earn more than three times his current income. Even more gains would have been made in the absence of state and local regulation. Admittedly, the minimum wage is just a small part of that flood of government intervention, but it does not help to stop it.

A policymaker and his economic adviser face two alternatives: Will they let some babies cry, and wait for mounting prosperity to feed them? Or will they feed some crying babies now with the food taken from other crying mouths? A related question is how many crying babies on one side justify taking food from the mouth of a baby on the other? (Make sure your numbers are correct!) Those are the value judgments that economists ultimately have to make when they take a policy stance in the minimum wage debate.

I suggest that leaving the minimum wage alone--or better, abandoning it--is both more conducive to prosperity and more easily defensible from a moral viewpoint.

READINGS

"America's 'Top Economists': What Explains Their Low Opposition to a Minimum Wage Increase in 2013?" by Jason Briggeman. Social Science Research Network Paper no. 2249040, April 11, 2013.

"Federal Regulation and Aggregate Economic Growth," by John W. Dawson and John J. Seater. *Journal of Economic Growth*, Vol. 18 (2013).

"Is There a Free-Market Economist in the House?" by Daniel B. Klein and Charlotta Stern. *American Journal of Economics and Sociology*, Vol. 66, No. 2 (April 2007).

Minimum Wages, by David Neumark and William L. Wascher. MIT Press, 2008.

"Minimum Wages: A Poor Way to Reduce Poverty," by Joseph J. Sabia. Cato *Institute Tax and Budget Bulletin* no. 70, February 27, 2014.

"Raise That Wage," by Paul Krugman. *New York Times*, February 17, 2013.

"Reasons for Supporting the Minimum Wage: Asking Signatories of the 'Raise the Minimum Wage' Statement," by Daniel B. Klein and Stewart Dompe. *Econ Watch Journal*, Vol. 4, No. 1 (January 2007).

"Revisiting the Minimum Wage-Employment Debate: Throwing Out the Baby with the Bathwater," by

David Neumark, J. M. Ian Salas, and William Wascher. *Industrial and Labor Relations Review*, forthcoming.

The Effects of a Minimum Wage Increase on Employment and Family Income, published by the Congressional Budget Office. Washington, D.C., February 2014.

"The Negative Effects of Minimum Wage Laws," by Mark Wilson. Cato Institute *Policy Analysis* no. 701, June 21, 2012.

"Walmart Needles *The Nation* about Low-Wage Intern Jobs, Hilarity Ensues," by Katherine Mangu-Ward. *Reason*, August 8, 2013.

Why Does the Minimum Wage Have No Discernible Effect on Employment? by John Schmitt. Center for Economic and Policy Research, February 2013.

1. Do you believe the author's premise that poverty caused by the "impersonal result of everybody's equal liberty" is more morally defensible than poverty caused by the so-called "coercion" of "people holding political power"?

2. What are some arguments why the reverse may be true?

"WORKING BACKWARDS: HOW EMPLOYMENT REGULATION HURTS UNEMPLOYED MILLENNIALS," BY GAIL HERIOT, FROM THE *HARVARD JOURNAL OF LAW AND PUBLIC POLICY*, SUMMER 2015

Think back, if you will, to Paris about eight years ago when the French government proposed reforms to its labor code that would have made it easier for employers to dismiss young employees. Millions hit the streets in protest. (1) Cars were torched. About 3,500 people were brought into custody, (2) most of them young, many of them unemployed. When the youth unemployment rate is officially at 21.6 percent, as it was in France at the time, (3) that is obviously a big problem. Just as obviously, the riots did not help.

By contrast, the proposed reforms just might have. Granted, they would have made first jobs less secure. An employer would have been able to hire an inexperienced employee, knowing that if it did not work out, he could end the relationship in the first two years, no questions asked--something that would not otherwise have been possible in France. (4) But the protesters were wrong to believe that a secure job was somehow being snatched away from them. Most did not have any job yet, and if they wanted to change that, they needed to recognize that laws making it hard for employers to terminate unsatisfactory employees or hire employees they want can discourage employers from hiring employees, particularly untested job applicants. (5)

In the end, the French government backed down. (6) As a result, some of those protesters are probably still unemployed. But while the employment outlook for young people here in the United States is not quite so grim, the further we move toward the famously protective French model, the worse we can expect it to be.

Our unemployment rate for those aged 20 to 24 was 11.5 percent in September--down from a year ago, but still almost three times the rate for those over the age of 35. Just to be clear, those figures both understate and over-state the problem. It overstates the problem in the sense that it includes only those in the job market. If you're in school, you're neither in the numerator nor the denomi-nator. It understates it in the sense that it excludes, among other things, those working part-time because part-time employment is all they are able to find, and those reluc-tantly pursuing additional educational credentials, only because they could not otherwise get a job. (7)

One hears a lot of overwrought talk these days about a so-called "war on women," but if there's a demo-graphic out there that we ought to be worrying about, it is young people, the perennial newcomers to the economy. Well-meaning employment laws primarily benefit those who already have jobs, often at the expense of those who do not. In that respect, they are like so many progressive policies. They help those on the second to last rung of the ladder, often at the expense of those on the bottom rung.

Many of these laws and policies may be attrac-tive or even justifiable when viewed individually, but when piled one on top of the other, they can become a difficult-to-surmount obstacle to youth employment. For low-skilled young people trying to get their first jobs, the most immediate threat may be the steep minimum wage hikes adopted recently in various cities. In Seattle, the minimum wage increase will be over 60 percent; in San Francisco, 39 percent; in Oakland, 36 percent. (8)

In the past, one of the only things that economists used to agree on was that minimum wage hikes kill jobs. These days, however, there are empirical studies going both ways, at least when it comes to modest increases. (9) But if the claim is that minimum wage hikes generally do not affect employment rates, that is an extraordinary claim, and extraordinary claims require extraordinary evidence. I would rank such a study as somewhat more plausible, but not much more plausible, than a study showing that mothers do not love their children, which if someone were to argue with me, I would smile politely and find someone with whom I could converse.

The notion that profit-making enterprises are insensitive to the price of unskilled labor should not be an easy sell. Not surprisingly, even the studies that purport to justify relatively modest hikes have problems. Perhaps the most famous of them, the Card and Krueger study, waited eight months before it looked to see the effects of an increase in minimum wages, and found that employment actually increased. (10)

But a study such as this may not take account of other ways that employers can reduce costs. And these changes may not take place over eight months. Last year, Applebee's announced, for example, that it would install tabletop tablets that allow customers to order and pay without the need for a waiter. (11) Those tablets won't be fully installed for a few more months. (12)

More fundamentally, the minimum wage increase studied by Card and Krueger was modest in comparison to those in Seattle, San Francisco, and

Oakland. (13) It also occurred at a time when the inflation rate was more than twice what it is today. It would be hard to argue that a 60 percent increase will not affect unemployment.

Recent college graduates face different hurdles, which are symbolized in the dreaded unpaid internship. In the book *Intern Nation: How to Earn Nothing and Learn Little in the Brave New Economy*, journalist Ross Perlin rails against this modern rite of passage, telling interns they have "nothing to lose but [their] cubicles." (14) Perlin urges interns to rise up and organize against this "simmering injustice." (15) Alas, he misses the point. These positions are not the result of some evil conspiracy. They evolved out of the modern legal and economic environment. Until that changes, a lot of twenty-five-year-olds will be living in their parents' basements.

There are some inevitable hurdles that new entrants to the workforce will confront. Young people even with great educational credentials are unknown quantities to employers and, hence, risky to hire, especially in a legal environment in which employee terminations can lead to costly legal disputes. School transcripts give very little insight into a job applicant's character and temperament. The proliferation of internships over the last thirty-five years is in part a response to these problems. Now, few would suggest doing away entirely with laws giving legal protection to existing employees. To be clear, that's not what I'm arguing here.

But the least we can do for struggling millennials is take a hard look at some of the ways in which employment laws, including employment discrimination laws, have backfired, doing no good or more harm than good for those who are supposed to benefit. It is not hard to find some of the backfires, ladies and gentlemen. The hard part is finding a fix that has a political chance of being adopted.

Let's start with Title VII's effect on small businesses. In theory, Title VII applies equally to hiring and firing. (16) In practice, however, all employers know that they are far more likely to be sued for firing than failing to hire, just as divorcing a spouse is more explosive than declining a first date.

This is not what supporters expected when the law was passed in 1964, a time when some newspapers were running "Help Wanted, White" ads. But consider the irony: The best way for employers to avoid being wrongly accused of a Title VII violation is to avoid hiring someone who could turn out to be litigious if things do not work out. That creates a perverse incentive to avoid hiring the first African American or the first woman in a particular business or department. Skittish small employers worry especially that if they need to terminate their first female employee, for example, they're going to look bad. A law that was intended to end discrimination in hiring, thus, ends up encouraging it instead. This is not an easy problem to solve, but we should not forget that the original Title VII initially applied only to employers with more than 100 employees before ratcheting down to 25, and now it has been amended to go down to 15. (17) State laws regulate even smaller employers. (18) This history may offer a lesson. There is certainly a case to be made that we would get less employment discrimination, rather than more, by increasing the minimum number of employees to 25 or higher.

Alternatively, one could amend the law to further limit the remedies as they apply to very small businesses. Another solution may be to allow prevailing employers or at least prevailing small employers to collect attorney's fees in most cases. It just so happens that the statute essentially says this, (19) but it has been interpreted by the courts to mean something other than that. (20)

Here's another high-impact area that needs reexamination: disparate impact liability. Ever since *Griggs v. Duke Power Co.* (21) in 1971, and truly before that, the EEOC has been telling employers that not only must they refrain from actual discrimination on the basis of race or sex, but they must also use hiring criteria that will yield equal or near equal results for women and minorities, regardless of whether they are consciously or unconsciously discriminating, unless they can prove business necessity. (22) For reasons hinted at by Justice Scalia in *Ricci v. DeStefano*, (23) I think it's unconstitutional, but more fundamentally, it's incoherent. *Every* job qualification has a disparate impact on some protected group. Disparate impact makes everything presumptively illegal. This drives everything underground. No employer can state its hiring criteria clearly without risking litigation. You can't even say, "We don't hire felons," and God help you if you try to administer any kind of standardized or non-standardized test to your job applicants. There is little or no evidence that, all things considered, this increases employment for racial minorities, and that is not because nobody has tried to show it.

There is some evidence in the case of the EEOC's policy on ex-offenders that it does the opposite. It encourages actual discrimination, as employers try to avoid applicant pools that they believe, rightly or wrongly, are likely to contain more ex-offenders. (24) So if you can hire from the elite college, rather than hiring from a part of town where there are more minorities, you have an incentive to do it.

In worldwide competition, we cannot offer employers the cheapest workforce or even the best educated, but we ought to be able to offer greater freedom and flexibility in selecting a team, so long as they are not motivated by race or sex. Meanwhile, too many millennials are stuck in internships by day, living in their parents' basements by night, or unemployed altogether. Here's to hoping they will understand a little more the reasons for their predicament and press for reform.

*Gail Heriot, Professor of Law, University of San Diego; Member, United States Commission on Civil Rights. These remarks were given at the Federalist Society National Lawyers Convention in Washington, D.C. on November 13, 2014.

1. Do you agree with the author's account? Why or why not?

2. Do you think the author overstates the extent to which employment discrimination legislation has hurt those it intended to help? In your opinion, can this argument be applied to the minimum wage?

"MAXIMUM DIVIDE ON MINIMUM WAGE: STUDIES ABOUND ON THE MINIMUM WAGE, BUT THE CONCLUSIONS DRAWN VARY GREATLY," BY JEANNE MEJEUR, FROM *STATE LEGISLATURES MAGAZINE*, MARCH 2014

To paraphrase an old joke, if there were only two economists left in the world, they would disagree about the minimum wage. Does it cost jobs or create jobs? It's a valid question, but the answer depends on who you ask.

Opponents of minimum wages contend that increased labor costs force businesses to cut staff, costing jobs. That sounds reasonable. Proponents of minimum wages argue that giving workers more disposable income puts money back into the economy, which in turn creates jobs. That makes sense, too.

So what's the answer?

Studies abound on the minimum wage. Some make common sense arguments while others use enough fancy math to dazzle any economist. Most studies are published by interest groups that either support or oppose a minimum wage, or from authors connected to such interest groups. If you read enough of these studies, you'll likely come to the realization that, almost without exception, they are trying to persuade you more than inform you.

THE PRO ARGUMENTS

Commonly used arguments supporting increases to the minimum wage follow.

1. Increases put more money into the pockets of low-income workers. According to a 2013 Congressional Research Service report, a single parent with two children who works full time at the current minimum wage would be earning around $15,000 and living at 76 percent of the federal poverty level. If the federal minimum wage was raised from the current $7.25 to $9.00 an hour, the same family would be at 94 percent of the poverty line.
2. Minimum wage increases shrink the gap between low-wage and higher-paid workers, lessening income inequality, both within individual businesses and in the larger economy.
3. Minimum wage increases put more money into the economy since low-income workers are more likely to spend their higher wages than are their higher paid counterparts, who are more likely to save them. This increased demand for goods and services tends to stimulate the economy, which, in turn, leads to job creation.
4. Higher minimum wages reduce turnover among low-wage workers. Lower turnover rates are a net positive for businesses, since high turnover increases training costs and results in lower productivity.

THE CON ARGUMENTS

Following are the most commonly cited arguments against minimum wage increases.

1. It results in job losses. Labor costs are the largest share of the budget for many businesses. Mandatory increases in hourly wages mean that businesses will be forced to cut jobs or reduce hours to maintain their bottom line. That could mean no income or reduced

income for low-wage workers.

2. There are better ways to address poverty, such as income tax credits for low-income workers or tax policies that encourage asset development and savings for low-income families.

3. Increased labor costs will be passed on to consumers through increased prices. Higher prices lead to decreased demand, which can have a depressive effect on the economy.

4. Increased labor costs result in lower profits for businesses. Lower profits mean that businesses have less money to put back into their enterprises for job creation and business expansion.

WHO EARNS MINIMUM WAGE?

According to the Bureau of Labor Statistics, based on 2012 figures:

- Around 3.6 million (or 4.8 percent) of the 75 million workers paid on an hourly basis earn $7.25 an hour or less.
- More than half of minimum wage workers are under the age of 25.
- Six percent of women and 3 percent of men earn minimum wages.
- The leisure and hospitality sector has the highest proportion of minimum wage workers.
- Louisiana, Oklahoma, Texas and Idaho have the highest percentage of minimum wage workers.
- Alaska, Oregon, California, Montana and Washington have the lowest percentage of minimum wage workers.

Source: The Bureau of Labor Statistics, 2012 data

So there you have it: There is no definitive study, no final answer. Whatever your opinion is on minimum wage, you can find a study that will back it up.

The last increase in the federal minimum wage was in 2009. In constant dollars, the minimum wage that was worth $7.25 in 2009 is now worth $6.67, due to the increased cost of living.

A seemingly indisputable fact is that, despite 22 increases in the 75 years since it was established in 1938, the federal minimum wage has not kept pace with inflation. In real dollars, the peak value of the federal minimum wage was in 1968, when the wage was set at $1.60. That would be $10.56 in today's economy, well above the current $7.25.

From a consumer's point of view, the average cost of a loaf of bread in 1968 was 22 cents, accounting for 14 percent of an hour's pay at the $1.60 minimum wage. The average cost of a loaf of bread in 2012 was $1.88, which accounts for 26 percent of an hour's pay at the current minimum wage. No matter how you slice it, the minimum wage hasn't kept up with inflation.

CONGRESS STALLS, STATES ACT

The lack of action on the federal level has prompted many states to consider increases to their state minimum wages.

All but five have adopted state minimum wages. Alabama, Louisiana, Mississippi, South Carolina and Tennessee have no state minimum wage, relying solely on the federal minimum wage for workers who are covered by the Fair Labor Standards Act. In addition, New Hampshire repealed its state minimum wage in 2011, but left a statutory reference to the federal minimum wage.

Nineteen states have set their state minimum wage to match the federal wage of $7.25, as have Guam, Puerto Rico and the U.S. Virgin Islands. Twenty-one states and the District of Columbia have established state minimum wages that are above the federal minimum wage. The highest state minimum wage is in Washington, at $9.32. California is set to surpass that in January 2016, when the state minimum wage will increase to $10.00 per hour.

Minimum wage continues to be a hot issue in state legislatures. As of Feb. 1, lawmakers had introduced legislation to increase the minimum wage in Delaware, Georgia, Iowa, Hawaii, Kentucky, Maryland, Massachusetts, Missouri, Nebraska, New Hampshire, New Jersey, New Mexico, New York, Oklahoma, Pennsylvania, Rhode Island, Tennessee, Utah, Washington and West Virginia. Delaware has already enacted an increase effective July 1, 2014, and Washington, D.C., passed an increase that is under review in Congress.

During the 2013 legislative session, lawmakers in 23 states and the District of Columbia introduced legislation to increase their state minimum wage, and bills passed in seven states. Four states--California, Connecticut, New York and Rhode Island--enacted minimum wage hikes that were signed into law.

Legislatures in Maine, New Jersey and New Mexico passed bills as well, but they were vetoed by the governors. Voters in New Jersey had the final say on the issue, however. They approved a constitutional amendment in the 2013 November election that raised the minimum wage and tied future increases to the cost of living.

FEDERAL PROPOSALS

The first minimum wage was set at $0.25 an hour in 1938 by the Fair Labor Standards Act. Congress has raised it 22 times since. In February, President Obama raised the minimum wage to $10.10 for federal contractors only. Meanwhile, in Congress, several bills on the minimum wage have been introduced. A quick look at these follows.

FAIR MINIMUM WAGE ACT OF 2013 (S. 460 AND H.R.1010)

- Increases to $8.20, $9.15, and $10.10 over three years
- Indexes subsequent increases
- Increases tipped wage to $3
- Indexes future tipped wage increases
- Fair Minimum Wage Act of 2013 (H.R. 3746)
- Increases to $8.50, $10, and $11 over three years
- Indexes subsequent increases

MINIMUM WAGE FAIRNESS ACT (S. 1737)

- Increases to $8.20, $9.15, and $ 10.10 over three years
- Indexes subsequent increases
- Increases tipped wage to $3
- Indexes future tipped wage increases
- Raises limits on business expenses

ORIGINAL LIVING AMERICAN WAGE ACT (H.R. 229)

- Adjusts federal minimum every four years
- Keeps minimum wage at 15 percent above poverty line

WAGES ACT (H.R. 650)

- Raises tipped wage to $3.75 and $5 over two years
- Indexes future tipped wage increases

CATCHING UP TO 1968 ACT OF 2013 (H.R.1346)

- Increases to $10.10
- Indexes subsequent increases
- Raises tipped wage to 70 percent of the minimum wage

THE INDEXING OPTION

States have taken a couple of different approaches to raising the minimum wage. The traditional method has been to establish a specific dollar amount with a specific effective date. Rhode Island's 2013 bill is an example of that approach. The General Assembly passed a law establishing $8.00 as the minimum wage beginning Jan. 1, 2014.

Sometimes a legislature will enact a multiple-step increase, as California lawmakers did last year. Its state minimum wage will increase to $9.00 on July 1, 2014, and jump to $10.00 on Jan. 1, 2016.

Other states have taken a different approach called indexing, which provides automatic annual increases based on the increased cost of living as determined by the Consumer Price Index. Eleven states have adopted indexed minimum wages since 2001. Interestingly, in 10 of the states, indexing was approved by voters. Vermont is the only state where the legislature approved indexing of the minimum wage.

Which approach is best? Both have their advantages and disadvantages.

INDEXING

- The minimum wage increases automatically without discussion or debate, avoiding legislative squabbles.
- Regular increases allow workers' wages to keep pace with inflation.
- It allows businesses to plan ahead for their labor costs,

BURGERNOMICS

Here's how many minutes it takes, earning minimum wage, to make enough to buy a burger around the world.

	Wages	Minutes
Australia	$16.88	18
France	$12.09	22
United Kingdom	$9.83	23
Japan	$8.17	31
United States	$7.25	35
Greece	$5.06	53
Brazil	$1.98	172
China	$0.80	183
India	$0.23	347

Source: "The Economist" magazine developed the Big Mac index in 1986 as a way to measure whether foreign currencies are at their "correct" level. It compares exchange rates in different countries to see if they result in the same purchasing power for an identical item--the burger. The ConvergEx Group, a global brokerage firm, adapted the news magazine's burgernomics to minimum wages in various countries to come up with this chart. Minimum-Wage. org provided the wage rates in "international dollars, " which is based on the U.S. dollar in 2009.

since they know in advance that wages will increase each year.
- The increases tend to be slightly larger overall, with an 18 cent an hour average annual increase.

STEP INCREASES

- Lawmakers can discuss and debate whether an increase is currently needed.
- Minimum wage bills often ignite battles as they go through the legislative process.
- Step increases take additional factors into account, such as the impact of natural disasters, high unemployment, or economic downturns, rather than looking only at inflation.
- Step increases tend to be larger when adopted, sometimes up to $1 an hour, but when averaged over the affected years, the increases are actually slightly smaller at an average of 16 cents an hour annually.

PUBLIC OPINION

Where does the public stand on the issue? In a Gallup poll conducted in November 2013, 76 percent of the public supported raising the federal minimum wage to $9.00 an hour. In the same poll, 69 percent of those asked supported an increase to $9.00 an hour and indexing future increases to the cost of living, to keep pace with inflation.

The same poll found that the level of support varies according to party affiliation but still has broad support among voters of all stripes. When asked whether they supported increasing the federal minimum wage to $9.00 an hour, 91 percent of Democrats, 76 percent of independents and 58 percent of Republicans said yes.

There was a bigger divide regarding indexing or "inflation-proofing" the minimum wage. Ninety-two percent of Democrats, 71 percent of independents and

43 percent of Republicans said they supported raising the federal minimum wage to $9.00 an hour and indexing future increases to inflation.

Pro or con, indexing or not, with minimum wage bills in Congress going nowhere, the issue continues to be hotly debated in state legislatures. It's likely voters in several states will see minimum wage ballot measures when they go to the polls for the mid-term elections this fall.

Reprinted with permission from the National Conference of State Legislatures.

1. Do you side with the "pro" or "con" side of the minimum wage raise debate? If so, what reason do you find to be most important in determining your position?

2. If you think the minimum wage should keep pace with the cost of living, do you think indexing or step increases are more effective to achieve this?

CHAPTER 2

WHAT THE GOVERNMENT AND POLITICIANS SAY

This chapter begins with an overview of the Fair Labor Standards Act. Like so many of the New Deal policies introduced by President Franklin Delano Roosevelt (FDR), the FLSA was part of a much larger social program to stabilize and, to some degree, rehabilitate capitalism in the wake of the Great Depression. As such, the minimum wage cannot accurately be described as a progressive measure. The real purpose of FLSA legislation was to manage dissent among the working poor and to maintain status-quo relations of production, rather than provide a living wage as a social entitlement of full-time work. As Dana Griffin points out, the minimum wage began as an attempt to keep workers "efficient and healthy"—presumably not due to altruistic motives!

Despite its compromised inception, the FLSA successfully staved off the most egregious of workplace violations such as wage theft and unpaid overtime. Subsequent amendments to the law have increased the scope of worker protections, and incrementally raised the minimum wage, though nowhere approaching a living wage after adjustment for inflation.

It is odd that Americans believe full-time work would provide a living wage. This is certainly a desirable and just state of affairs. However, generally speaking, this has never been the case. From the plantation to the sweatshop, our economy has literally been built on exploitative labor practices.

Despite this, politicians who support raising the minimum wage often do so to pledge an allegiance to middle-class values and morality—perhaps the only meaningful relic of an economically-gutted middle class. Although free-market ideology and the influence of business interests will no doubt insure minimum wage increases are kept low, there is mounting evidence that the fight for better wages is fostering a labor movement with a more radical agenda.

"SUMMARY OF THE FAIR LABOR STANDARDS ACT," BY DANA GRIFFIN, FROM *CHRON.COM*

Congress passed the Fair Labor Standards Act on June 25, 1938. Its job was to eliminate labor conditions that led to low standards of living. The act, known as FLSA, was originally enacted during the Great Depression. The belief was that maintaining higher living standards helped to keep workers efficient and healthy.

DEFINITION

FLSA sets minimum wage, overtime pay, equal pay, record keeping and child labor standards. The provisions originally applied to private sector employees only, but now generally apply to public sector as well. Some specific cities and towns still have exempt employees. The Wage and Hour Division enforces FLSA for private employment, state and local governments and federal employees from the Library of Congress, United State Postal System, Postal Rate commission and the Tennessee Valley Authority. The U.S. Office of Personnel Management handles other executive branch employees and U.S. Congress enforces it for legislative branch employees.

SCOPE

All employees of any enterprise that matches one of the following three criteria are covered under FLSA. First, if the business has an annual gross volume of sales of at least $500,000. Second, if the business is a hospital or otherwise engaged in caring for the sick, elderly or mentally disabled or if it is a educational institution including preschools, elementary, secondary schools or higher education institutions. Third, employees are covered if the enterprise is an activity of a public agency. FLSA covers domestic service workers such as housekeepers, cooks, nannies and groundskeepers if their annual wages are at least a yearly minimum set by the Social Security

Administration--$1,500 in 2007--or if they work more than eight hours in one week.

FUNCTION

FLSA sets the federal minimum wage standard, although many states set their minimum requirements higher. In 2008, federal minimum wage was $6.55, and it rose to $7.25 in July 2009. Overtime pay must be at least 1.5 times an employee's regular hourly pay and applies to any additional hours worked past 40 in a normal workweek. The FLSA does not regulate all employment practices, including severance or sick pay; meal or rest periods; holidays or vacations; pay raises or bonuses; or premium pay for weekend or holiday work.

PROVISIONS

The FLSA sets a lower minimum for workers younger than age 20 during their first three months of employment with a given employer: $4.25 per hour as of 2009. Employers must not replace over-aged workers with youth workers in order to pay lower wages. They are also prohibited from reducing hours, wages or benefits in order to hire younger workers.

CONSIDERATIONS

Some individuals are exempt from the minimum wage standards in specific situations. These include student learners, such as vocational education students, full-time students in retail or service establishments or those that work in institutes of higher education. Employers may also pay lower wages to employees whose productivity is limited due to physical or mental disability, including those related to age or injury.

1. Do you think the FLSA is helpful to workers? Or did it merely offer small concessions to ensure business as usual?

2. What do you think about the lower minimum wage set for workers younger than twenty?

"HISTORY OF CHANGES TO THE MINIMUM WAGE LAW," BY THE US DEPARTMENT OF LABOR, 2014

ADAPTED FROM *MINIMUM WAGE AND MAXIMUM HOURS STANDARDS UNDER THE FAIR LABOR STANDARDS ACT*, 1988 REPORT TO THE CONGRESS UNDER SECTION 4(D)(1) OF THE FLSA.

Early in the administration of the FLSA, it became apparent that application of the statutory minimum wage was likely to produce undesirable effects upon the economies of Puerto Rico and the Virgin Islands if applied to all of their covered industries. Consequently on June 26, 1940, an amendment was enacted prescribing the establishment of special industry committees to determine, and issue through wage orders, the minimum wage levels applicable in Puerto Rico and the Virgin Islands. The rates established by industry committees could be less than the statutory rates applicable elsewhere in the United States.

On May 14, 1947, the FLSA was amended by the Portal-to-Portal Act. This legislation was significant because it resolved some issues as to what constitutes compensable hours worked under FLSA. Matters involving underground travel in coal mines and make-ready practices in factories had been decided earlier in a number of U.S. Supreme Court decisions.

Subsequent amendments to the FLSA have extended the law's coverage to additional employees and raised the level of the minimum wage. In 1949, the minimum wage was raised from 40 cents an hour to 75 cents an hour for all workers and minimum wage coverage was expanded to include workers in the air transport industry. The 1949 amendments also eliminated industry committees except in Puerto Rico and the Virgin Islands. A specific section was added granting the Wage and Hour Administrator in the U.S. Department of Labor authorization to control the incidence of exploitative industrial homework. A 1955 amendment increased the minimum wage to $1.00 an hour with no changes in coverage.

The 1961 amendments greatly expanded the FLSA's scope in the retail trade sector and increased the minimum for previously covered workers to $1.15 an hour effective

September 1961 and to $1.25 an hour in September 1963. The minimum for workers newly subject to the Act was set at $1.00 an hour effective September 1961, $1.15 an hour in September 1964, and $1.25 an hour in September 1965. Retail and service establishments were allowed to employ fulltime students at wages of no more than 15 percent below the minimum with proper certification from the Department of Labor. The amendments extended coverage to employees of retail trade enterprises with sales exceeding $1 million annually, although individual establishments within those covered enterprises were exempt if their annual sales fell below $250,000. The concept of enterprise coverage was introduced by the 1961 amendments. Those amendments extended coverage in the retail trade industry from an established 250,000 workers to 2.2 million.

Congress further broadened coverage with amendments in 1966 by lowering the enterprise sales volume test to $500,000, effective February 1967, with a further cut to $250,000 effective February 1969. The 1966 amendments also extended coverage to public schools, nursing homes, laundries, and the entire construction industry. Farms were subject to coverage for the first time if their employment reached 500 or more man days of labor in the previous year's peak quarter. The minimum wage went to $1.00 an hour effective February 1967 for newly covered nonfarm workers, $1.15 in February 1968, $1.30 in February 1969, $1.45 in February 1970, and $1.60 in February 1971. Increases for newly subject farm workers stopped at $1.30. The 1966 amendments extended the fulltime student certification program to covered agricultural employers and to institutions of higher learning.

In 1974, Congress included under the FLSA all no supervisory employees of Federal, State, and local governments and many domestic workers. (Subsequently, in 1976, in *National League of Cities v. Usery*, the Supreme Court held that the minimum wage and overtime provisions of the FLSA could not constitutionally apply to State and local government employees engaged in traditional government functions.) The minimum wage increased to $2.00 an hour in 1974, $2.10 in 1975, and $2.30 in 1976 for all except farm workers, whose minimum initially rose to $1.60. Parity with nonfarm workers was reached at $2.30 with the 1977 amendments.

The 1977 amendments, by eliminating the separate lower minimum for large agricultural employers (although retaining the overtime exemption), set a new uniform wage schedule for all covered workers. The minimum went to $2.65 an hour in January 1978, $2.90 in January 1979, $3.10 in January 1980, and $3.35 in January 1981. The amendments eased the provisions for establishments permitted to employ students at the lower wage rate and allowed special waivers for children 10 to 11 years old to work in agriculture. The overtime exemption for employees in hotels, motels, and restaurants was eliminated. To allow for the effects of inflation, the $250,000 dollar volume of sales coverage test for retail trade and service enterprises was increased in stages to $362,500 after December 31, 1981.

As a result of the Supreme Court's 1985 decision in *Garcia v. San Antonio Metropolitan Transit Authority et.al.*, Congress passed amendments changing the application of FLSA to public sector employees. Specifically, these amendments permit State and local governments to compensate their employees for overtime hours worked with compensatory time off in lieu of overtime pay, at a rate of 1 ½ hours for each hour of overtime worked.

The 1989 amendments established a single annual dollar volume test of $500,000 for enterprise coverage of both retail and no retail businesses. At the same time, the amendments eliminated the minimum wage and overtime pay exemption for small retail firms. Thus, employees of small retail businesses became subject to minimum wage and overtime pay in any workweek in which they engage in commerce or the production of goods for commerce. The minimum wage was raised to $3.80 an hour beginning April 1, 1990, and to $4.25 an hour beginning April 1, 1991. The amendments also established a training wage provision (at 85% of the minimum wage, but not less than $3.35 an hour) for employees under the age of twenty, a provision that expired in 1993. Finally, the amendments established an overtime exception for time spent by employees in remedial education and civil money penalties for willful or repeated violations of the minimum wage or overtime pay requirements of the law.

In 1990, Congress enacted legislation requiring regulations to be issued providing a special overtime exemption for certain highly skilled professionals in the computer field who receive not less than 6 and one-half times the applicable minimum wage.

The 1996 amendments increased the minimum wage to $4.75 an hour on October 1, 1996, and to $5.15 an hour on September 1, 1997. The amendments also established a youth sub minimum wage of $4.25 an hour for newly hired employees under age 20 during their first 90 consecutive calendar days after being hired by their employer;

revised the tip credit provisions to allow employers to pay qualifying tipped employees no less than $2.13 per hour if they received the remainder of the statutory minimum wage in tips; set the hourly compensation test for qualifying computer related professional employees at $27.63 an hour; and amended the Portal-to-Portal Act to allow employers and employees to agree on the use of employer provided vehicles for commuting to and from work, at the beginning and end of the work day, without counting the commuting time as compensable working time if certain conditions are met.

The 2007 amendments increased the minimum wage to $5.85 per hour effective July 24, 2007; $6.55 per hour effective July 24, 2008; and $7.25 per hour effective July 24, 2009. A separate provision of the bill brings about phased increases to the minimum wages in the Commonwealth of Northern Mariana Islands and in American Samoa, with the goal of bringing the minimum wages in those locations up to the general federal minimum wage over a number of years.

1. Does this historical background support the conclusion that the minimum wage will continue to increase incrementally?

"MAKING WORK PAY: THE CASE FOR RAISING THE MINIMUM WAGE," BY ROBERT B. REICH, FROM THE U. S. DEPARTMENT OF LABOR, MARCH 1996

FACT SHEET

Americans know a raise in the minimum wage is one way to help make work pay. For many working Americans an increase in the minimum wage will make the difference between living in poverty and not. Furthermore, a higher minimum wage -- a floor to ensure workers that they're getting a fair deal for their efforts -- provides a foothold into the middle class for many other families.

THE PROBLEM: THE MINIMUM WAGE IS WORTH LESS THAN IT USED TO BE

The Federal minimum wage is currently $4.25 per hour. Adjusted for inflation, the value of the minimum wage has fallen by nearly 50 cents since it was last increased in 1991, and is now 29% lower than it was in 1979. If left unchanged, its real value will be at a forty-year low by January 1997.

Raising the minimum wage is one way to make work pay. A recent study concluded that the decline in the real value of the minimum wage since 1979 accounts for 20% of the rise in wage inequality for men, and 30% for women (see DiNardo, Lemieux & Fortin). According to the Bureau of Labor Statistics, 3.66 million workers paid by the hour earn at or below the minimum wage. An increase in this living wage is a strong response to the stagnant incomes that many of these workers face.

MANY ADULTS RELY ON THE MINIMUM WAGE AS A LIVING WAGE

Contrary to popular opinion, the average worker affected by an increase in the minimum wage is not just a teenager flipping hamburgers. Only one in fourteen is a teenage student from a family with above average earnings.

The fact is, almost two-thirds of minimum wage workers are adults, and four in ten are the sole bread winner of their family.

INCREASING THE MINIMUM WAGE LIFTS FAMILIES OUT OF POVERTY

Twenty percent of those living on the minimum wage the last time it was raised in 1991 were in poverty, and an additional 13% were near poverty. In 1993, the President expanded the Earned Income Tax Credit (EITC), which raised income for 15 million families, helping many working families move above the poverty line. Yet to complete the goal of insuring that fulltime working families are out of poverty, we need to raise the minimum wage. Recent analysis by the Economic Policy Institute and preliminary work by the Department of Health and Human Services suggests that 300,000 people would be lifted out of poverty if the minimum wage was raised to $5.15 per hour. This figure includes 100,000 children who are currently living in poverty.

The current poverty line for a family of 4 is $15,600. A family of 4 with one worker earning $4.25 an hour and working full-time year round ($8,500) would receive a tax credit of $3,400 under the 1996 provisions of the EITC, will collect food stamps worth $3,516, and will pay $650 in payroll taxes. This family would end up $834 below the poverty line. On the other hand, for a family of 4 with one worker earning $10,300 (a full-time year round worker at $5.15 per hour), the EITC would provide the maximum tax credit ($3,560), food stamps would provide $2,876, and they would pay $788 in payroll taxes. The increase in the minimum wage -- along with EITC and food stamps -- would lift this family out of poverty.

WHAT A MODERATE INCREASE IN THE MINIMUM WAGE WOULD MEAN FOR WORKERS

The President's proposal to raise the minimum wage by $.90 would generate $1800 in potential income for minimum wage workers. Based on expenditure patterns of an average family, $1800 would buy:
- Seven months of groceries
- One year of health care costs, including insurance premiums, prescription drugs, and out-of-pocket costs
- Nine months' worth of utility bills
- More than a full-year's tuition at a 2-year college
- Basic housing costs for almost 4 months

MANY WORKING WOMEN DEPEND UPON THE MINIMUM WAGE

Fifty nine percent of workers earning from $4.25 to $5.14 per hour are women; of those, 72 percent are adults 20 years old or over. The President's proposal to increase the minimum wage would raise wages of more than 5.7 million working women. This includes more than 950,000 African-American women and 760,000 women of Hispanic origin. Single heads of households, who are often women, represent over one-fifth of all families who currently rely on the earnings of a worker making $4.25 to $5.14 per hour.

A MODERATE INCREASE IN THE MINIMUM WAGE DOES NOT COST JOBS

The standard criticism of the minimum wage is that it raises employers' costs and reduces employment opportunities for teenagers and disadvantaged workers. However, several studies have found that the last two increases in the minimum wage had an insignificant effect on employment. Furthermore, an extension of the time-series studies that had previously been used to claim that raising the minimum wage decreases employment, no longer finds a significant impact.

In a recent review of the literature, Professor Richard Freeman of Harvard, a widely respected labor economist, wrote: "At the level of the minimum wage in the late 1980s, moderate legislated increases did not reduce employment and were, if anything, associated with higher employment in some locales. "

In discussing the minimum wage, Robert M. Solow, a Nobel laureate in economics at the Massachusetts Institute of Technology, recently told the New York Times, "The main thing about (minimum wage) research is that the evidence of job loss is weak. And the fact that the evidence is weak suggests that the impact on jobs is small."

AMERICANS WANT AN INCREASE IN THE MINIMUM WAGE

The American public supports increasing the minimum wage by a solid margin. Nearly every survey finds overwhelming support for raising the minimum wage. For example, a national poll conducted in January 1995 for the Los Angeles Times found that 72% of Americans backed an increase in the wage, confirming a December 1994 Wall Street Journal/NBC News survey that found raising the minimum wage is favored by 75%.

Despite expected criticism in some corners, the minimum wage has traditionally had bipartisan support. In 1989, the minimum wage increase passed the House by a vote of 382 to 37 (with 135 Republicans voting for the bill), and 89 to 8 in the Senate (with the support of 36 Republicans).

Currently, ten states and the District of Columbia have minimum wages that exceed the Federal minimum wage (Alaska, Connecticut, Hawaii, Iowa, Massachusetts, New Jersey, Oregon, Rhode Island, Vermont and Washington). Delaware is expected to pass legislation that will raise its minimum wage on April 15, 1996. Hawaii's minimum wage is $5.25 an hour and Massachusetts will match this in January 1997; New Jersey's is $5.05.

THE MINIMUM WAGE: MYTH AND REALITY

The federal minimum wage now stands at $4.25 per hour. A person who works full-time all year long at that wage earns only $8500 in a year. The buying power of the minimum wage is already 29 percent lower than in 1979 --

and if left unchanged, will be at its lowest point in 40 years by January 1997. To restore that buying power and to make work pay, the President has challenged Congress to raise the minimum wage. But the debate has been muddied by several myths that anti-minimum wage forces repeat at every opportunity.

Myth: The only Americans working for the minimum wage are teenagers.
Reality: 63 percent of minimum-wage workers are adults age 20 or over. (Source: Bureau of Labor Statistics)

Myth: Minimum wage workers don't support families.
Reality: The last time the federal minimum wage was increased, the average minimum wage worker brought home 51 percent of his or her family's weekly earnings, (Source: Analysis of Census Bureau's Current Population Survey by Professors David Card and Alan Krueger)

Myth: Raising the minimum wage hurts the poor by causing job loss.
Reality: Nearly 10 million working Americans would get a pay raise if the minimum wage is increased to $5.15 per hour. As Nobel Prize-winning economist Robert Solow said, " [T]he evidence of job loss is weak. And the fact that the evidence is weak suggests that the impact on jobs is small. " (Source: *New York Times*, January 12, 1995)

Myth: The only study showing that raising the minimum wage does not cost jobs was a study funded by the U.S. Labor Department.

Reality: One major study -- conducted in 1992 and financed by Princeton University and the University of Wisconsin -- was published by two Princeton University economists. One of those economists later joined the Labor Department. (Source: *Washington Post*, January 11, 1995) Furthermore, a similar conclusion has been reached by at least ten other independent studies.

Myth: Raising the minimum wage will have a negligible impact on people's lives.

Reality: A 90-cent per hour increase in the minimum wage means an additional $1,800 for a minimum wage earner who works full-time, year round -- as much as the average family spends on groceries in more than 7 months. (Source: Bureau of Labor Statistics)

Myth: Increasing the minimum wage has always been a bitter, partisan issue that only Democrats have supported.

Reality: In 1989, the last time the minimum wage was increased, the House of Representatives vote in favor of the proposal was 382 to 37, and the Senate vote was 89 to 8. Indeed, Senator Dole said at the time, " [T]his is not an issue where we ought to be standing and holding up anybody's getting a 30 to 40 cents an hour pay increase, at the same time that we're talking about capital gains. I never thought the Republican Party should stand for squeezing every last nickel from the minimum wage. "

(Source: *Congressional Quarterly Almanac 1989*)

MAKING WORK PAY: QUESTIONS AND ANSWERS ON RAISING THE MINIMUM WAGE

With unemployment at its lowest level in years, should we be tinkering with the minimum wage? Won't an increase in the minimum wage hinder the creation of new jobs?

The minimum wage is currently valued at 29 % lower in real terms than it was in 1979.

A number of recent studies have found that a moderate rise in the minimum wage has little, if any, affect on job creation starting at such a low level. In fact, "The impact of a minimum wage rise on jobs is small, " the New York Times quoted Nobel Laureate Robert Solow as saying. The Times also reported that economists agree that a minimum wage rise will lift the incomes of low wage workers.

Isn't the minimum wage poorly targeted to people in poverty? The Democratic Leadership Council reports that a number of minimum wage workers are in households with earnings higher than the median worker. Wouldn't a rise in the minimum wage just help middle class teenagers?

Although some people who earn the minimum wage are teenagers, almost two-thirds are adults age 20 and older. The average minimum wage worker brings home about half of his or her family's earnings. Increasing the minimum wage will help these workers to make up for lost ground due to inflation -- it will help make work pay.

The minimum wage provides a foothold into the middle class. A family with two fulltime year round workers would earn $20,600 a year with a $5.15 minimum wage.

Wouldn't a rise in the minimum wage hurt minorities and the disadvantaged due to job loss?

As the New York Times reported, most economists agree that raising the minimum wage increases the incomes of low wage workers, which more than offsets any effect on jobs. Further, studies of minimum wage increases fail to show disproportionate impacts for minority youth.

Additionally, public support for a minimum wage increase is strong. A January 1995 Los Angeles Times poll found that 72% of Americans back an increase, confirming a December 1994 Wall Street Journal/NBC News poll that found that 75% of adults favored a rise in the minimum wage.

How many workers are affected by a rise in the minimum wage?

An estimated 10 million hourly paid workers earn between $4.25 and $5.14, and would directly benefit from the President's proposal to increase the minimum wage.

How can you contemplate a rise in the minimum wage with a new Congress intent on getting government off the backs of business?

The minimum wage has historically enjoyed bipartisan support. Sens. Dole and Kassenbaum, Speaker

Gingrich and Rep. Goodling voted for the last minimum wage increase to $4.25 an hour in 1989.

Governors across the country are fighting against unfunded mandates. Isn't the minimum wage an unfunded mandate on businesses and states?

The minimum wage is not a new unfunded mandate. In fact, given the erosion of the value of the minimum wage over the last 15 years it is now much less of a mandate on businesses and the public sector than it used to be.

What do you say to all the businesses that say they will lose profit and possibly go bankrupt if the minimum wage is raised? Aren't you just antagonizing the business community by proposing a minimum wage increase?

Inflation has eroded the minimum wage so much that it is currently at its second lowest level since the 1950s. The economy has been very strong, but wages have not grown as much as they need to for the middle class to keep up.

The Clinton Administration has pursued economic policies to put our fiscal house in order, laying the foundation for the current economic expansion. But the problem is that low-wage and middle class workers have not shared fully in this recovery.

1. This piece was written almost 20 years ago, yet the argument that a rise in the minimum wage yields increased unemployment persists. What might account for this argument's tenacity?

2. In your opinion, what is the best reason against prioritizing the minimum wage issue politically?

"HOUSE AND SENATE INTRODUCES BILLS TO INCREASE MINIMUM WAGE TO $9.80," FROM *RAISE THE MINIMUM WAGE*, JUNE 2012

BILL INTRODUCTION FOLLOWS NATIONAL DAY OF ACTION TO RAISE THE MINIMUM WAGE

Washington, DC – Today the U.S. Senate and House of Representatives introduced the Fair Minimum Wage Act of 2012, companion bills that would raise the federal minimum wage to $9.80 by 2014 and impact millions of working Americans. The introduction follows a National Day of Action in which thousands of workers and their supporters held approximately 50 events in 30 cities in a call to raise the minimum wage, boost job creation and address the nation's growing economic inequality.

The bills are sponsored by Senator Tom Harkin (D-IA), chair of the Health, Education, Labor and Pensions Committee in the Senate, and Representative George Miller (D-CA), ranking member of the House Committee on Education and the Workforce. The National Employment Law Project applauded the legislation, highlighting how it will improve pay for millions of struggling workers and their families, and boost spending at a time when the economy is suffering from weak consumer demand.

"Millions of the nation's lowest-paid workers are putting in long hours and working multiple jobs, yet are still struggling to afford basic expenses," said Christine Owens, executive director of the National Employment Law Project. "Raising the minimum wage, which now provides full-time earnings of barely $15,000 a year, is an important step to make sure work provides economic opportunity and security for working families. We applaud Senator Harkin and Representative Miller for their leadership on this crucial issue."

The Fair Minimum Wage Act of 2012 would raise the federal minimum wage from the current rate of $7.25 to $9.80 per hour by 2014, and it would provide for annual increases to the rate in future years to keep pace with the rising cost of living – a key reform known as "indexing," which ten states have already adopted. The Harkin-Miller bills would also raise the minimum wage for tipped workers from its current low rate of $2.13 per hour, where it has been frozen since 1991, to $6.85 over five years. Thereafter, it would be fixed at 70 percent of the full minimum wage.

As underscored in Tuesday's nationwide Day of Action, paychecks for millions of workers have been falling, even as corporate profits reach record levels. The Bureau of Labor Statistics reported last month that average weekly paychecks fell by 1.7 percent in the final quarter of last year. Congress has voted to raise the minimum wage only three times in the last 30 years, and today, the real value of the minimum wage is 30 percent lower than in 1968.

Recent polling reveals broad public support for raising the minimum wage: A national poll of 2012 voters earlier this year found that nearly three in four likely voters (73 percent) support increasing the minimum wage to $10 and indexing it to inflation. In 2008, then-presidential candidate Barack Obama pledged to raise the minimum wage to $9.50 by 2011, but no action has been taken. Presidential candidate Mitt Romney in January of this year stated his support for raising the minimum wage, but later claimed that no raise was necessary.

Restoring the minimum wage would play an important role in bolstering the nation's economic recovery. The Commerce Department reported this month that retail sales fell 0.5 percent in June, the third straight month of consistently declining sales in the retail industry. Higher wages for the nation's lowest-paid workers would put money in the pockets of people who are likely to spend that money immediately, boosting demand for goods and services in the local economy.

The Economic Policy Institute estimates that the Harkin-Miller proposal would generate more than $25 billion in new consumer spending, which would result in more than 100,000 new full-time jobs. EPI also estimates the Harkin-Miller bill would increase wages for nearly 30 million Americans – roughly one-fifth of the workforce – as raising the wage floor improves pay for workers who earn at or just above the minimum wage.

A new report from the National Employment Law Project also finds that, contrary to misimpressions, 66 percent of low-wage workers are employed by large corporations, not small businesses. It also found that more than 70 percent of the biggest low-wage employers have recovered from the recession and are enjoying strong profits – yet wages remain stagnant for their frontline employees.

1. This bill, like other federal minimum wage bills that came before and after, was not enacted. Why do you think it failed to be passed by Congress?

2. After the information you have read, do you think this bill is political maneuvering, or an honest attempt to expedite economic recovery for a broader swath of Americans?

CHAPTER 3

WHAT THE COURTS AND LEGAL COMMUNITY SAY

As the neo-populist "Fight for $15" labor movement gains traction, the courts are increasingly becoming the preferred venue for corporate attempts at pushback. Many indicators suggest these corporations will lose.

In the landmark case of Seattle-based *West Coast Hotel v. Parish* (1937), the Supreme Court established a new precedent for ruling on the side of workers. In that case, the court ruled five to four that minimum wages did not violate the Fourteenth Amendment of the Constitution. Prior to this, the courts viewed wages as freely negotiated contractual agreements, the defining characteristic of the so-called "Lochner Era." Interestingly, the court upheld a law intended to guard against "pernicious effects on the morals" of women and children, but which did not guarantee them a living or even fair wage.

Seattle's current fifteen-dollar municipal minimum wage law is the nation's highest, and continues to face legal challenges. In this chapter, we'll examine a suit in which companies doing business at the Seattle airport challenged the jurisdiction of the city of SeaTac, whose citizens passed a fifteen-dollar minimum wage via ballot initiative. According to the plaintiffs, the Port of Seattle exercises authority over the airport, so businesses there aren't subject to SeaTac's laws. The court upheld Proposition 1, however, claiming that the plaintiffs failed to prove that higher wages interfere with airport operations.

Fast-food workers have recently begun organizing for higher wages, so we can expect more lawsuits in that industry. Matt Tripp reports on how these profitable companies will fight tooth and nail to avoid paying employees higher wages. Fortunately for fast-food workers, the industry's challenges rely on arguments that the courts seldom uphold.

"LANDMARK CASES: *WEST COAST HOTEL V. PARRISH* (1937)," BY ALEX MCBRIDE, FROM PBS.ORG

In West Coast Hotel v. Parrish (1937), the Supreme Court ruled, 5-4, that Washington State could impose minimum wage regulations on private employers without violating the Constitution's Fourteenth Amendment. The case sounded the death knell of the so-called "Lochner era," during which the Court held that the Fourteenth Amendment protects substantive economic rights against the state, such as the right to freely negotiate contracts and wages. West Coast Hotel ruled that no such right exists and that a state may constitutionally restrict the terms of private contracts when protecting the welfare of its citizens.

In 1932, Washington State passed a law entitled "Minimum Wages for Women." It called for minimum wages for women and children as a means to combat "pernicious effects on their health and morals" and provided for a special commission, with input from industry and the public, to determine appropriate minimum wage levels. Elsie Parrish, a chambermaid at the West Coast Hotel, later sued the hotel in a state court claiming that it had not paid her the law's minimum wages. Parrish sought the balance of her income between what she was actually paid and the minimum wage (set at $14.50 per week of 48 hours). West Coast Hotel defended by arguing that the law was unconstitutional. The state court agreed and ruled for the hotel. Parrish appealed to the Washington Supreme Court, which reversed the lower court's ruling and directed that damages be paid to Parrish. West Coast Hotel appealed to the U.S. Supreme Court, which reviewed the case in 1936 and issued its opinion in 1937.

The Supreme Court, in a 5-4 decision written by Chief Justice Charles Evans Hughes, ruled that the minimum wage law did not violate the Constitution's Fourteenth Amendment and Parrish was entitled to damages. The Fourteenth Amendment's Due Process Clause provides that no state "shall deprive any person of life, liberty, or property, without due process of law." West Coast Hotel alleged that because the minimum wage law prevented employers and employees from freely negotiating wages, it restrained "liberty" of contract without due process of the law. In response, the Court flatly declared that the "Constitution does not speak of freedom of contract" and that such a freedom is thus "a qualified, and not an absolute, right" under the Fourteenth Amendment. The Court argued that while the Fourteenth Amendment bans arbitrary deprivation of life, liberty, and property by the state (or protects "procedural" due process, e.g., a right to a fair trial), it does not prohibit the states' ability to "reasonably" regulate the terms of certain activities for the public good (does not protect "substantive" due process, e.g., the basic right to freely contract).

The Court next ruled that the minimum wage law did not violate "procedural" due process because it was a "reasonable," not arbitrary, regulation. Though it interfered with contractual freedoms between "adults," the Court held that it was now reasonable -- given changing social and economic conditions -- for governments to set a floor under which wage levels could not drop. Ultimately, the Court held that the minimum wage law was constitutional because it reasonably regulated contracts to protect the health and welfare of workers.

West Coast Hotel v. Parrish, sensibly as it reads today, was a radical and controversial departure in 1937. The decision directly overturned the landmark decision Adkins v. Children's Hospital (1923), which ruled that laws fixing terms of employment contracts violated the Due Process Clause because the clause protects a substantive right to freely contract labor ("substantive" due process). Although the Court's sudden rejection of "substantive" due process has sometimes been attributed to political pressures, because the decision was issued right after President Franklin Roosevelt proposed a "court-packing scheme" that would have added "anti-Lochner" justices to the Court to protect New Deal legislation, the Court actually voted on the case prior to Roosevelt's announcement of his proposal. The exact chronology of events aside, historians debate whether and to what degree the day's political climate affected Justice Josephus Roberts' unexpected switch -- sometimes referred to as "the switch in time that saved nine" -- to the pro-New Deal wing of the Court. West Coast Hotel's position on economic regulations remains settled law today.

1. Minimum wage laws have a paternalistic history, as seen in this 1937 court case that aimed to protect a woman from her employer. Do you think this is an ongoing problem?

2. Do you think the Lochner era's insistence on "contractual" agreements ignored power relations in the workplace? How?

"AIRLINE INDUSTRY ALERT: WASHINGTON STATE SUPREME COURT FINDS SEATAC ORDINANCE INCREASING MINIMUM WAGE TO $15 AN HOUR ENFORCEABLE AT AIRPORT," BY DOUGLAS HALL, FROM FORDHARRISON, AUGUST 25, 2015

Executive Summary: In a 5-4 decision, the Washington State Supreme Court has held that Proposition 1 - an ordinance that increased the minimum wage within the city of SeaTac for employees in the hospitality and transportation industries to $15 an hour - is also enforceable at the Sea-Tac Airport. *Filo Foods, LLC v. City of SeaTac*, (Wash. Aug. 20, 2015). This means that Proposition 1 may now be applicable to employees of airline service providers and, in certain circumstances, to employees of air carriers themselves, at the airport.

BACKGROUND

In June 2013, a group supporting an increase in the minimum wage for hospitality and transportation workers at Sea-Tac Airport circulated a petition among the voters in the city of SeaTac (within which the airport is located) to put Proposition 1 on the ballot. In addition to increasing the hourly minimum wage, Proposition 1 would require covered employers to provide paid sick leave, offer additional hours to part-time employees before hiring new staff, and ensure that tips were retained by the workers performing the services. It also would impose obligations on successor employers to retain certain workers for a period of time. Proposition 1 would apply to employees of airline service providers but not employees of certificated air carriers to the extent that the airline was performing services for itself.

Proposition 1 narrowly passed, and several affected employers subsequently challenged the law, claiming it was preempted by state and federal law. Although the trial court upheld Proposition 1 generally, it held that the ordinance could not be enforced at the airport because, under state law, the city could not exercise jurisdiction or control over the airport. The trial court also found that one aspect of Proposition 1, relating to penalties for retaliating against employees for exercising rights under the ordinance, was preempted by the National Labor Relations Act. The parties appealed different aspects of the trial court's decision. On August 20th, the Washington Supreme Court reversed the trial court on these two points, but otherwise affirmed the trial court's ruling.

THE HIGH COURT'S DECISION

First, the court held that Proposition 1 could be applied at the airport, and was not in conflict with state law concerning the Port of Seattle's jurisdiction over the airport, because the Port had not shown that Proposition 1 would "interfere with airport operations." The court then rejected the argument that Proposition 1 was preempted by federal labor law (in whole or in part) under the Machinists or Garmon doctrines. The court further held that Proposition 1 was not preempted by the Airline Deregulation Act because it was not sufficiently related to airline services and prices, finding that Proposition 1 was a "generally applicable" law rather than one directly targeted at the airline industry. Finally, the court found that Proposition 1 did not violate the dormant Commerce Clause. The dissent disagreed with the majority's conclusion that Proposition 1 could be applied at the airport under state law, as it felt that the Port had exclusive jurisdiction over the airport.

THE BOTTOM LINE:

Although the majority stated that it was "upholding" Proposition 1 in its entirety, it did not address the practical impact of its decision, such as whether and to what extent employers would have to comply with the requirements of Proposition 1 retroactively, to the ordinance's January 1, 2014 effective date. The majority's decision also made some statements regarding the scope of the Port's authority that could have an impact on currently pending litigation involving a challenge to the Port's own efforts to increase wages and benefits at the airport. We will monitor the case with respect to these and any other developments.

1. Although the court upheld Proposition 1, do you foresee any practical obstacles to its enforcement?

2. Under the logic of those who oppose hikes to the minimum wage, would we not expect to see job losses at the airport? But is this a likely outcome? Why or why not?

"WHY THE COURTS WON'T SAVE FAST FOOD COMPANIES FROM THE $15 MINIMUM WAGE," BY MATT TRIPP, FROM *EATER.COM*, AUGUST 14, 2015

HOW PENDING LITIGATION IN SEATTLE COULD IMPACT THE FUTURE OF FIGHT FOR $15

July marked another victory for the Fight for $15 labor movement, with New York's Fast Food Wage Board recommending a mandatory minimum wage increase to $15 per hour for all New Yorkers working for major fast-food chains — those with 30 or more locations in the state. The law would be phased in over the next six years, and when all is said and done, it would increase the current minimum wage by more than 70 percent. New York Governor Andrew Cuomo, under whose authority the Wage Board was convened, made no bones about the proposed law directly targeting the fast-food industry: He noted the fast-food sector is the largest employer of low-wage workers and, notwithstanding billion-dollar profits, "nowhere is the income **gap more extreme and obnoxious** than in the fast-food industry."

If New York's Labor Commissioner accepts the recommendation, New York will join Seattle, San Francisco, and Los Angeles as one of the few places in America where fast-food workers are paid $15 per hour. Both the New York proposal and Seattle's ordinance specifically target fast-food restaurants, albeit in slightly different ways. While Seattle's ordinance merely requires large fast-food chains to begin paying the $15 per hour minimum wage sooner than independent businesses, the New York proposal applies exclusively to large fast-food chains.

Not surprisingly, the fast-food industry is doggedly resisting the wage increases. The Seattle ordinance was challenged in court within a week of its enactment, and some New York franchise owners are already contemplating a lawsuit if the state passes the recommended wage hike. This raises an obvious question: **Who's going to win, workers or fast-food corporations?**

The answer can likely be found in the lawsuit surrounding Seattle's ordinance, which is the paradigm case in this most recent installment in the Fight for $15. The Seattle lawsuit represents the primary legal arguments the fast-food industry will likely rely on when it challenges local minimum wage increases elsewhere. As a result, the outcome of that suit will not only predict the likelihood of New York franchisees' success if they decide to sue; it may also very well determine the future of the Fight for $15 movement.

THE FRANCHISE BUSINESS MODEL

Before digging into fast-food's minimum wage lawsuits, it's important to define fast-food's most common business structure — the franchise. Sometimes simply referred to as a chain, a franchise is a business structure in which a large business (the franchisor) contracts with smaller businesses (the franchisees) to open outlets and sell the franchisor's brand of products. Many of the larger fast-food franchises, such as McDonald's, Burger King, KFC, and Subway, have outlets throughout the nation and even the entire world.

Generally, each franchisee is independently owned and operated. Fast-food workers are typically considered **employees of the franchisee and not the franchisor**. Thus, franchisees are responsible for paying their own labor costs. And therein lies the rub — the fast-food industry argues that fast-food franchises are virtually indistinguishable from small, locally-owned restaurants, and thus, should be treated the same. But that's not the case under either the Seattle ordinance or the New York proposal, both of which consider the number of employees and outlets associated with the franchise — as a whole — in determining whether fast-food chains are small businesses that qualify for preferable treatment under the law.

THE SEATTLE ORDINANCE

Seattle enacted its $15 per hour minimum wage ordinance in June 2014, and it distinguishes between local outposts of large franchises — those employing more than 500 employees nationwide — and small mom-and-pop-shops. The two different kinds of businesses have different grace periods to adjust to the increased labor costs: Large Seattle franchisees must begin paying the $15 per hour minimum wage by 2017, while "smaller businesses" have until 2021 to meet the $15 mark. Seattle justifies the ordinance's different treatment of large franchises on the grounds that they have greater resources than small business, and as a result, are capable of coming into compliance with the ordinance in a shorter period of time.

But the International Franchise Association (IFA) and a group of five individual franchisee owners and managers quickly responded by filing suit against the city. The crux of IFA's claims against Seattle is that the city's new ordinance **unconstitutionally discriminates against large franchises** by requiring franchisees to come into compliance with the ordinance more quickly than small, locally-owned business. This type of discrimination, where the government treats some types of businesses differently than others, is sometimes termed "economic discrimination."

At the outset of the case, IFA requested a preliminary injunction: It asked the court to prohibit Seattle from enforcing the ordinance's three-year compliance period against franchises until the discrimination case was resolved. In order to determine whether a preliminary injunction was warranted, the court assessed the likelihood of IFA succeeding on its constitutional claims — it ultimately determined that IFA was unlikely to succeed on its claims at trial, and it therefore **refused to grant the injunction**. Importantly, the court did not actually decide the case in ruling on IFA's request; the case is still very much alive. However, the court's denial of the injunction is supported by a bevy of case law rejecting claims of economic discrimination. Such claims are generally rooted in two provisions of the United States Constitution: the Equal Protection Clause of the Fourteenth Amendment and the Dormant Commerce Clause. IFA argues that Seattle's ordinance violates both constitutional provisions, but the court disagrees:

The case is still very much alive, but the court denied IFA's request for a preliminary injunction, rejecting its claims of economic discrimination.

PROVISION ONE: THE EQUAL PROTECTION CLAUSE

The Fourteenth Amendment Equal Protection Clause was adopted in 1868 largely to prevent discrimination against individuals — in this case, newly-freed slaves. Since its enactment, the Clause has been properly extended to protect individuals and corporations against other forms of discrimination, including discrimination based on gender, alienage and nationality, and most recently, sexual orientation. Although the application of the Equal Protection Clause is not necessarily limited to only these groups, courts are **extremely reluctant to extend the Clause's protections much further**. And nowhere is this reluctance stronger than in cases of alleged economic discrimination.

The Equal Protection Clause allows laws that discriminate along economic lines, as long as there is some "rational basis" for the law. Although the term "rational basis" looks innocuous, it can actually be understood as the atomic bomb of constitutional law, typically destroying all of the plaintiff's claims. Laws that discriminate on the basis of economics **will always be upheld** if there is any conceivable basis for its existence. In a famous 1981 case, the United States Supreme Court applied rational basis review to a Minnesota law that prohibited the sale of milk in certain types of plastic containers. The Minnesota legislature claimed the law was meant to protect the environment, but the dairy industry presented "impressive supporting evidence" that the law would actually hurt the environment. The law was nevertheless upheld because, as the Court put it, under rational basis review, "States are not required to convince the courts of the correctness of their legislative judgments."

It therefore comes as no surprise that the Seattle court rejected IFA's Equal Protection argument. The court acknowledged the similarities between franchisees and small, locally-owned business but focused more heavily on **several important distinctions** between the two types of businesses. Unlike other business entities, franchisees benefit from their franchisors' trademarks, national advertising, market power, and trade secrets. With these distinctions in mind, the court determined that Seattle's ordinance is constitutional because the city can reasonably expect franchises to be capable of coming into compliance with the ordinance more rapidly.

PROVISION TWO: THE DORMANT COMMERCE CLAUSE

IFA did not fare any better under its Dormant Commerce Clause argument. The Dormant Commerce Clause is aimed at prohibiting state and local governments from engaging in economic protectionism: If a local law directly discriminates against out-of-state businesses, it will almost always be constitutionally invalid. If the law instead only imposes an incidental burden on interstate commerce, it will be upheld as long as the burden is not clearly excessive in relation to the law's purpose. Seattle's ordinance applies to all businesses, regardless of where they are headquartered: a Seattle-based franchise is treated the same under the city's minimum wage ordinance as a Delaware-based franchise. But IFA argues that because over 96 percent of the franchises operating in Seattle are in fact out-of-state businesses, the ordinance directly discriminates against interstate commerce.

However, the court determined that even this enormous disparity in the number of in-state versus out-of-state franchises is insufficient to establish direct discrimination. Furthermore, the court held that any burden imposed on interstate commerce by Seattle's minimum wage ordinance is not clearly excessive in relation to the ordinance's vital purpose, which is to give workers a means to support themselves without relying on state social services.

THE NEW YORK PROPOSAL

So what does all this mean for New York's proposal? Not surprisingly, fast-food industry attorneys told NBC News that a lawsuit challenging the New York law would be based on the same economic discrimination arguments raised in the Seattle case. Again, the Seattle case is still working its way through the courts, currently pending appeal in the 9th Circuit. But the judge's denial of IFA's request for a preliminary injunction suggests that the fast-food industry will **ultimately lose.**

There is no reason to suspect that constitutional challenges to the New York proposal, should it become law, would come out any differently. The constitutionality of economic discrimination is deep-rooted in Supreme Court precedent, and trial courts have no choice but to stay the course. Furthermore, recent history suggests that New York trial courts are particularly quick to strike down exploitative labor practices.

It could take years for these cases to work their way through the courts. In the meantime, it appears the fast-food industry will continue to pay workers low wages, reap record profits, and allocate a portion of those profits to litigation aimed at stymieing efforts to obtain a livable wage for the industry's workers.

1. Do you think franchises should be treated as national businesses, even if each location is independently owned and operated?

2. All indications show that the fast food industry will lose this lawsuit. But do you think this will cause the fast-food industry to change for the better? Is it likely they will draw talented employees away from nutritionally-superior establishments, neighborhood cafes, etc.?

ADVOCACY GROUPS FOR AND AGAINST THE MINIMUM WAGE INCREASE

Chapter Four begins by tracing the history of minimum wage laws in the United States. As Oya Aktas explains, the terms and intellectual underpinnings of the minimum wage debate were established long ago, around the beginning of the twentieth century. Her conclusions highlight the subtle discrimination embedded in labor law and its application.

Next, we'll examine perspectives on increasing the minimum wage from advocates both for and against this legal action. The conservative Minimum Wage Team argues against it, deploying the familiar rhetoric that low-skilled workers act against their long-term interests by supporting higher minimum wages. The team also claims that higher minimum wages will not benefit those earning the least, since a majority of minimum wage workers provide only supplementary income for their households. This view has been widely discredited by other studies.

On the pro side, some argue that the minimum wage should be increased for pragmatic reasons. Will Kramer's article for the business publication *Risk Management* warns that since the Occupy Wall Street movement brought the issue of inequality into mainstream discourse, unusually high CEO-to-median pay averages can hurt a company's bottom line. Kramer recommends that companies address income inequality, if only to improve their public image. This is strategically similar to corporate attempts to appear more environmentally friendly through superficial change, also known as "greenwashing."

"THE INTELLECTUAL HISTORY OF MINIMUM WAGE AND OVERTIME," BY OYA AKTAS, FROM THE *WASHINGTON CENTER FOR EQUITABLE GROWTH*, SEPTEMBER 10, 2015

The rapid growth of the "Fight for $15" minimum wage movement and President Barack Obama's changes to overtime regulations have sparked new rounds of debate over the economic consequences of an increased overtime pay threshold and a higher minimum wage. Advocates of overtime and wage hikes argue these policies protect workers from exploitation and improve job quality. Opponents insist these regulations will hurt workers in the long run, as they will inflict a burden on companies that will be forced to cut jobs. These concerns are nothing new—this debate dates back to the early 20th century, before the minimum wage even existed in the United States and when overtime pay was unheard of.

At the end of the 19th century, economists such as John Bates Clark preached that markets, if left to their own devices, would function at equilibrium levels with the best possible distribution of resources. Rapid industrialization created the Gilded Age of American wealth, and people credited the free market with their increased prosperity. (1) But along with increasing growth, industrialization also sharpened economic inequalities and made certain groups particularly vulnerable to exploitation. Debates over hour and wage limits focused on which groups required labor protections and the best mechanisms for protecting these groups.

Labor regulations began in the 1890s as state-level maximum hour and minimum wage protections, which the U.S. Supreme Court repeatedly struck down. Federal standards were not created until four decades later, when president Franklin Delano Roosevelt and his Secretary of Labor, Frances Perkins, guided the Federal Labor Standards Act into law. This issue brief details the arguments that shaped hour and wage limits in the early 20th century.

WOMEN'S MAXIMUM HOURS

U.S. legal historians usually describe the beginning of the 20th century as the "Lochner Era," a 32-year period characterized by the Supreme Court's attempt to protect the free market through its constant repeal of labor laws. The Supreme Court actually was discriminatory in its protection of the free market—although it consistently blocked labor laws that applied to men, the high court allowed restrictions on women's employment. The Supreme Court passed distinct rulings for men and women by emphasizing different doctrines for the two sexes. For men, the court consistently upheld freedom of contract; for women, the court privileged police powers.

The Supreme Court's gender discrimination began with cases concerning maximum hour limits. In *Lochner v New York (1905)*, the namesake of the Lochner Era, the court justified its decision to strike down the 1895 Bakeshop Act—which placed hour limits on New York bakers—with the freedom of contract doctrine. Freedom of contract comes from the due process clause of the Constitution, which says that no person shall be "deprived of life, liberty, or property without due process of law." At the time, justices interpreted due process to mean that individuals should be free from restraint except to guarantee the same freedoms to others, and that government could not restrict people's ability to acquire future property. (2) Limiting the hours that New York bakers worked, proponents argued, took away their liberty to choose the terms of their employment and limited the money they could earn, so maximum hour laws violated freedom of contract.

Just three years later, the Supreme Court set a different standard for women. In *Muller v Oregon* (1908), it upheld a 1903 Oregon law that prohibited women from working more than 10 hours a day. The court argued that women's freedom to contract was superseded by the police powers doctrine, which allows government regulation for the purpose of promoting health, safety, morality, and the general welfare of the public. (3) The court found that "as healthy mothers are essential to vigorous offspring, the physical wellbeing of woman is an object of public interest." (4) In other words, protecting women's reproductive health was more important than respecting their freedom to contract. Women were also seen as fragile, vulnerable, and lacking the skills necessary to effectively bargain for wages and working conditions, and therefore unable to exercise their freedom of contract. These sex-specific discussions about government-imposed hour limits set the stage for a new conversation: the passage of state minimum wages.

WOMEN'S MINIMUM WAGES

In 1912, Massachusetts became the first state to pass a minimum wage law that applied only to women and children. Thirteen more states (along with DC and Puerto Rico) followed in the next 11 years. (5) These legislatures passed a patchwork of legislation with a range of wage limits and enforcement mechanisms. States such as Massachusetts created wage commissions to determine industry-specific minimum wages and enforced standards through public shaming, publishing the names of companies that did not comply with the regulations. In contrast, states such as Arkansas set two cross-industry minimum wages for women: experienced women were paid $1.25 a day while inexperienced women only got $1. (6)

The police powers doctrine justified minimum wages for women, but said nothing about how they affected industries. To justify minimum wages on the industry side, academics used the parasitic industries argument. Originally developed by the British economists Beatrice and Sidney Webb in the late 19th and early 20th centuries, the parasitic industries argument says that businesses who focused on short-term profit maximization instead of long-term efficiency tend to pay workers unlivable wages. Workers receiving these sweatshop wages become a burden to society, since they have to rely on charity or other family members for subsistence. To fix the problem, companies have to either amend their practices to consider the long-term welfare of the company and the workers, or exit the market. (7)

Women's minimum wage laws grew out of gender norms supporting women's protection, but at the same time, racial biases led to laws that neglected women of color. Because minimum wage legislation was usually industry-specific, industries such as domestic work, agriculture, retail, and laundry—all dominated by African American workers—were often excluded from regulation. One case in point: The Wage Board in the District of Columbia set a weekly rate for laundry workers that was $1 lower than the across-the-board minimum adequate weekly wage of $16 it has previously chosen. The board explained that since 90 percent of laundry workers were African American, "the lower rate was due to a crystallization by the conference of the popular belief that it cost colored people less to live than white." (8) By not extending equal minimum wage protections to African American women, minimum wage laws reinforced their lower economic status. (9)

In the next decade, legal changes in women's status, paired with the economic optimism of the Roaring Twenties, brought a big shift in minimum wage legislation. Ratified in 1920, the 19th Amendment granted Women's Suffrage. Shortly after, in a victory for more equal gender standards but a loss for labor protections, the Supreme Court issued a ruling that struck down women's minimum wage laws across the country. In *Adkins v Children's Hospital (1923)*, the court overturned the 1918 law that created D.C.'s Wage Board, which had set minimum wages for women employed in laundries and food-serving establishments.(10) Reasoning that women were now politically empowered to advocate for themselves in the free market, the Court privileged freedom of contract over police powers and nullified minimum wage laws in the United States.

This optimism about the competitiveness of the free market did not last long. Once the Great Depression hit, people lost faith in the fairness of the U.S. economy. The failure of the banks cultivated distrust of large corporations. People were afraid tat business concentration hurt competition and created unfair trusts. The new popular economic narrative of economists such as Joan Robinson and Edward Chamberlain said that imperfect and monopolistic competition dominated the market. This unfair competition gave businesses a huge advantage, which they used to exploit labor. Public opinion shifted toward seeing government intervention not as redistribution but rather as reestablishing a competitive market. (11)

THE FAIR LABOR STANDARDS ACT

In this rapidly shifting political and economic climate Franklin D. Roosevelt won the 1932 elections and appointed Frances Perkins as his Secretary of Labor. With decades of experience advocating for labor rights as a social worker and later as Roosevelt's Secretary of Labor when the future president was governor of New York, Perkins accepted the federal cabinet office on the condition that Roosevelt would commit to supporting her reform platform, which included hour limits and minimum wages for both women and men. Perkins' platform originally appeared in the National Industrial Recovery Act, which tried to improve working conditions through voluntary industrial participation. Under the proposed law, industries would be able to form alliances, which previously violated anti-trust laws, if they complied with maximum hour and minimum wage standards. (12) In return, participating companies could display a Blue Eagle emblem in their stores, brandishing their patriotism and commitment to post-Great Depression recovery. (13) In *Schechter Poultry Corp. v United States (1935)*, however, the Supreme Court struck down the law, drawing the ire of Roosevelt and forcing Perkins to find a new way to pass labor reform.

Out of growing frustration with the Supreme Court's challenges to his policies, Roosevelt came up with a plan to pack the court. He set off a campaign to reform the Supreme Court so he could appoint additional members to the court who would vote in line with his New Deal reforms. Faced with this existential threat and greater public support for labor laws, in 1937 the Supreme Court ruled in favor of

Washington state's minimum wage law for women in *West Coast Hotel Co. v Parrish*. The court's ruling de-emphasized the freedom of contract, reversing its 1923 decision and opening the door for future minimum wage legislation. (14)

Following the Supreme Court decision, Perkins and Roosevelt sent a maximum hour and minimum wage bill to Congress. The original draft of the bill had called for industry-specific, regionally variant minimum wages to account for regional differences in prices and cost of living. As the bill made its way through Congress, two more opposition groups emerged: unions and northern industries. Unions feared that government-imposed wage and hour restrictions would undermine their influence in collective bargaining. Northern industries opposed regionally specific wages for fear that industries would follow the cheap labor south. To appease these two groups, Roosevelt and his Democratic allies in Congress tweaked the bill to make it more popular. (15) Roosevelt appeased the unionists' fears in his State of the Union address by emphasizing that more desirable wages should continue to be the responsibility of collective bargaining. Lawmakers suggested a national minimum wage to satisfy northerners, but set the wage low enough to appease southerners.

In its final form, the Fair Labor Standards Act of 1938 mandated a 44-hour workweek, scheduled to decrease to 40 hours in three years, with time-and-a-half overtime wages. The new law also created a minimum wage of 25 cents an hour, set to increase by 5 cents a year to reach 40 cents an hour by 1945. The original law was not universal. It included exemptions for agricultural, domestic, and some union-covered industries—once again, mostly industries dominated by African Americans. (16) Since the law lacked a mechanism for automatically increasing wages beyond 1945, it has been updated over the decades to increase wages and broaden industry (and racial) coverage. In the most recent revision to the Fair Labor Standards Act in 2009, the federal minimum wage was increased to $7.25 an hour.

CONCLUSION

The intellectual history of maximum hours and minimum wages is a story of debates over which groups should be protected from exploitation and what form this protection should take. Concerns over women's health, ambivalence toward African American rights, and advocating for unorganized workers dominated the debate at different points. As social views changed, so did economic policies. Today, women account for two-thirds of minimum wage earners and people of color account for two-fifths. (17) Studying the history of the minimum wage should compel policymakers to question how social priorities influence different groups, who is considered worthy of protection, and to what extent their welfare is considered. By implementing effective maximum hour and minimum wage regulations, policymakers can protect vulnerable workers' standard of living to encourage productivity, push companies to increase their efficiency, and consequently cultivate long-term equitable growth.

1. Was the original FLSA too compromised to provide real gains to workers?

2. According to the author, "studying the history of the minimum wage should compel policymakers to question how social priorities influence different groups, who is considered worthy of protection, and to what extent their welfare is considered." How would you answer these questions?

"THE IMPACT OF A $12 FEDERAL MINIMUM WAGE," BY THE MINIMUM WAGE TEAM, FROM *MINIMUMWAGE.COM*, NOVEMBER 13, 2015

The "Raise the Wage Act," introduced by Sen. Patty Murray (D-CA) and Rep. Bobby Scott (D-VA) in March 2015 would raise the federal minimum wage by 66 percent to $12 an hour. The legislation received a high-profile backer this fall in Democratic presidential candidate Hillary Clinton.

Proponents say that such a boost will reduce poverty without reducing jobs. But the academic evidence suggests otherwise. Economists from American and Cornell University studied the 28 states that raised their minimum wages between 2003 and 2007 and found no associated reduction in poverty. And, last year, the nonpartisan Congressional Budget Office (CBO) drew on the best available minimum wage research to analyze the impact of a $10.10 federal minimum wage and concluded that 500,000 employees would lose their jobs if the legislation came into effect.

In this new analysis, Drs. William E. Even and David Macpherson, economists from Miami University and Trinity University, respectively, use the same methodology as the CBO and conclude that 770,000 jobs would be lost if this legislation mandating a $12 minimum wage were enacted.

The analysis also explores the reasons why minimum wage increases have historically had such little success in decreasing poverty. The analysis finds that the average household income of those affected by the $12 legislation is $55,800. That's largely because, as the analysis reveals, 60 percent of those affected by the hike are secondary or tertiary earners in their household.

Presidential primary candidate Hillary Clinton has argued for a minimum wage increase as part of her policy platform to boost the middle class. But this analysis shows that those with household incomes between $35,000 and up to $100,000 would bear a large portion (43%) of the job loss from this higher minimum wage.

JOB LOSS

In the table below [*editor's note: table is reproduced on the opposite page*], the economists use Current Population Survey (CPS) data to identify the number of employees in each state who would be affected by a $12 minimum wage. Using the CBO methodology, they estimate the amount of job loss that would occur if the minimum wage increase were enacted. In total, they conclude that approximately 770,000 jobs would be lost nationwide at a $12 minimum wage.

NUMBER AFFECTED AND EMPLOYMENT LOSS BY STATE

STATE	EMPLOYMENT LOSS	NUMBER AFFECTED
ALABAMA	12,672	436,264
ALASKA	896	36,663
ARIZONA	15,085	560,480
ARKANSAS	9,792	288,450
CALIFORNIA	36,868	2,745,977
COLORADO	9,665	351,603
CONNECTICUT	3,260	203,048
DELAWARE	2,503	71,367
DISTRICT OF COLUMBIA	64	13,978
FLORIDA	46,357	1,669,425
GEORGIA	32,675	972,185
HAWAII	854	81,875
IDAHO	6,606	162,522
ILLINOIS	28,462	909,686
INDIANA	25,488	655,922
IOWA	12,964	296,424
KANSAS	12,307	277,724
KENTUCKY	14,504	385,656
LOUISIANA	14,937	415,619
MAINE	3,707	115,096
MARYLAND	2,981	308,409
MASSACHUSETTS	758	165,938
MICHIGAN	30,266	851,156
MINNESOTA	10,525	389,068
MISSISSIPPI	10,406	264,235

STATE	EMPLOYMENT LOSS	NUMBER AFFECTED
MISSOURI	21,909	527,664
MONTANA	2,674	90,815
NEBRASKA	4,657	165,500
NEVADA	6,745	250,388
NEW HAMPSHIRE	4,102	103,620
NEW JERSEY	15,605	619,732
NEW MEXICO	4,035	150,605
NEW YORK	33,409	1,310,273
NORTH CAROLINA	36,922	1,037,398
NORTH DAKOTA	2,050	55,431
OHIO	32,029	946,626
OKLAHOMA	10,812	298,454
OREGON	3,086	231,217
PENNSYLVANIA	40,430	1,055,487
RHODE ISLAND	2,560	77,950
SOUTH CAROLINA	14,824	455,845
SOUTH DAKOTA	1,769	69,287
TENNESSEE	26,275	628,054
TEXAS	91,645	2,673,048
UTAH	10,171	248,033
VERMONT	558	32,134
VIRGINIA	24,223	661,336
WASHINGTON	3,561	314,605
WEST VIRGINIA	5,188	168,778
WISCONSIN	24,547	496,486
WYOMING	1,616	44,333

Other minimum wage proponents, most notably presidential candidate Hillary Clinton, have backed the proposal as part of a policy package to help middle class. However, in the table below, the economists show that those households with incomes between roughly $35,000 and $100,000 would bear a large proportion of the job loss, losing approximately 43 percent of the 770,000 lost jobs.

EMPLOYMENT LOSS BY HOUSEHOLD INCOME

FAMILY INCOME	EMPLOYMENT LOSS	# AFFECTED	% OF EMPLOYMENT LOSS
Up to $34,999	316,801	11,347,257	41%
$35,000 – $99,999	329,122	10,583,633	43%
$100,000 or More	124,082	3,410,980	16%

Using CPS data, the economists also identify which demographics would be hardest hit by this job loss. They find that it would disproportionately impact black Americans, who would suffer 18 percent of the lost jobs despite being 13 percent of the U.S. population.

EMPLOYMENT LOSS BY RACE

RACE	EMPLOYMENT LOSS	# AFFECTED
White	584,403	19,026,468

RACE	EMPLOYMENT LOSS	# AFFECTED
Black	129,212	4,232,848
Other Race	56,390	

FAMILY INCOME AND FAMILY STATUS

The CPS also allows the economists to identify the income and family characteristics of those who would be affected by the wage hike. Contrary to the claims of minimum wage proponents, who argue that the minimum wage needs to be raised to help those in poverty, the analysis finds that the average family income of those affected by the proposed wage hike is $55,800 – around three times the federal poverty line.

FAMILY INCOME OF AFFECTED EMPLOYEES

STATE	AVERAGE
ALABAMA	$48,181
ALASKA	$69,365
ARIZONA	$51,459
ARKANSAS	$42,235
CALIFORNIA	$57,441
COLORADO	$60,571
CONNECTICUT	$80,132
DELAWARE	$57,702
DISTRICT OF COLUMBIA	$69,667
FLORIDA	$48,771
GEORGIA	$49,526
HAWAII	$70,118

IDAHO	$46,912
ILLINOIS	$69,481
INDIANA	$53,124
IOWA	$52,585
KANSAS	$53,436
KENTUCKY	$42,387
LOUISIANA	$51,146
MAINE	$54,313
MARYLAND	$78,635
MASSACHUSETTS	$84,474
MICHIGAN	$54,773
MINNESOTA	$70,135
MISSISSIPPI	$45,113
MISSOURI	$57,157
MONTANA	$43,828
NEBRASKA	$54,477
NEVADA	$50,371
NEW HAMPSHIRE	$75,658
NEW JERSEY	$75,709
NEW MEXICO	$49,589
NEW YORK	$62,636
NORTH CAROLINA	$43,853
NORTH DAKOTA	$62,401
OHIO	$55,118
OKLAHOMA	$52,235
OREGON	$48,953
PENNSYLVANIA	$62,981

STATE	AVERAGE
RHODE ISLAND	$62,731
SOUTH CAROLINA	$48,210
SOUTH DAKOTA	$57,170
TENNESSEE	$48,353
TEXAS	$49,792
UTAH	$57,369
VERMONT	$62,362
VIRGINIA	$65,459
WASHINGTON	$58,382
WEST VIRGINIA	$51,555
WISCONSIN	$62,462
WYOMING	$55,504
UNITED STATES	$55,769

Further examination of the CPS data helps explain this apparent paradox. The economists find that roughly 60 percent of those affected by the proposed minimum wage hike are secondary or tertiary earners in their families. In other words, most minimum wage earners supplement family incomes rather than drive them. In fact, only 9 percent of those affected by the wage hike are single parents.

FAMILY STATUS OF THOSE AFFECTED BY $12

STATE	SINGLE ADULT	SINGLE PARENT	MARRIED SOLE EARNER	MARRIED DUAL EARNER	LIVING W/ FAMILY OR RELATIVE
UNITED STATES	21.37%	9.09%	8.91%	20.14%	40.49%

METHODOLOGY

Drs. Even and Macphersons' estimates rely on data from the Current Population Survey from January through December 2014. The Current Population Survey (CPS), jointly sponsored by the Bureau of Labor Statistics and the U.S. Census Bureau, contains data obtained from monthly interviews with approximately 60,000 house-holds from all 50 states and the District of Columbia. The data provides weights that allow researchers to estimate labor market statistics at the national or state level. For example, the CPS is the primary data source for estimates of the national and state unemployment rate, as well as hours worked and hourly wages.

When a household is selected for inclusion in the CPS, it is included for four consecutive months, then excluded for 8 months, and then it returns for an additional 4 months. Earnings data is collected from household members only in their 4th and 8th interview when they are considered part of an "outgoing rotation group" (ORG). Because earnings data is essential to our analysis of minimum wage effects, they rely on data collected from households who are part of a CPS-ORG between January and December 2014.

To project the distribution of wages in 2020 without passage of the new legislation, they assume that every potentially affected worker has wage growth of 2.9 percent annually until 2020 and that the labor force will grow by 0.86 percent annually. These assumptions are based on the CBO's own forecast of wage growth for low skill workers in their study of the employment effects of minimum wage hikes, and their projection of employment growth. Also, for any state that indexes their minimum wage for inflation, they assume that the minimum wage would grow by 2.1 percent annually based on the CBO forecast of inflation for 2015 and 2020. For any worker who earned at or above the minimum in the year of the survey (2014) and whose predicted wage in 2020 was below the projected minimum in their state of residence, they increase their wage to the state's minimum in 2020. For workers who earned up to $.25 below the minimum in the year of the survey, they increase by the amount that the state's minimum wage would increase based on current law. This means, for example, that a person who earned $.15 less than the minimum wage in 2014 would still earn $.15 below the state's new minimum in 2020.

ESTIMATING AFFECTED WORKERS AND EMPLOYMENT LOSS

After generating the forecast of the 2020 distribution of wages reflecting wage growth and the effects of indexing on the minimum wage, they identify workers who would be affected by the new law mandating a $12.00 minimum as those with wages between the predicted state minimum wage legislated for 2020 and the proposed minimum ($12). They also include those workers who theyre slightly below (up to $.25) the old and new minimum.

To estimate the number of affected workers, they estimate the number of affected workers for 2020 based on the 2014 data. They estimate the number of affected workers by summing their earnings weights (adjusted for labor force growth through 2020) and dividing the total by 12 (the number of months of data). To estimate employment loss, for each affected worker they compute:

$$L = e *(\text{Proposed Min Wage} / \text{Min Wage 2020} - 1)$$

where e is an assumed elasticity of employment with respect to changes in the minimum wage, Min Wage 2020 is the minimum wage currently legislated for 2020 and Proposed Min Wage is the $12.00 minimum that is being proposed for 2020. To estimate the aggregate employment loss in the economy, they use adjusted earnings weights to sum L across workers. They also follow the Congressional Budget Office (2014) and use an elasticity of 0.15 for non-teenagers and 0.45 for teenagers.

1. This article argues that most minimum wage earners contribute supplementary income to otherwise middle-class households. Does the evidence the author provides convince you of this?

2. If the scenario above proves accurate, would job losses be an acceptable trade-off for increased wages?

"RAISING MINIMUM WAGE GOOD FOR PUBLIC HEALTH, NOT JUST WALLETS: ADVOCATES CALL FOR FEDERAL INCREASE," BY KIM KRISBERG, FROM *THE NATION'S HEALTH*, MARCH 2015

LAST YEAR, Minnesota legislators successfully enacted a raise in the minimum wage, taking Minnesota from one of the lowest-paying minimum wage states to one of the highest. State Health Commissioner Edward Ehlinger described the move as the greatest legislative victory of the year.

"I'd argue that it was the biggest public health achievement in that legislative session--and probably in the four years I've been health commissioner," Ehlinger, MD, MSPH, an APHA member, told *The Nation's Health*. "Even the tobacco tax increase the year before is not as powerful as the minimum wage increase."

In August, thousands of low-wage workers in Minnesota experienced the first in a series of incremental wage increases that will eventually reach $9.50 per hour by mid-2016. Prior to the new law, the state's minimum wage for large employers was just $6.15 an hour-- significantly lower than the federal minimum wage of $7.25. Small employers will raise their minimum wage to $7.75 by mid 2016, as well.

In the run-up to the vote, Ehlinger and his colleagues at the Minnesota Department of Health played an active role in educating policymakers and the public on the health benefits of raising the minimum wage and the evidence-based associations between income and health status.

Just a few months before the vote, the health department released a white paper on income and health, which showed that income is not only tied to health, but to the factors that create the opportunities for better health, such as safe homes, nutritious foods and good schools.

"If you look at the conditions that impact health, income is right at the top of the list," Ehlinger said. "Anything we can do to help enhance economic stability will have a huge public health benefit. This is a major public health issue."

The movement to raise the minimum wage has experienced great momentum in recent years, especially at the state and local levels. In 2014, lawmakers in 10 states and Washington, D.C., enacted minimum wage increases, while voters in four states approved ballot measures. A number of localities have taken action as well--for example, Seattle's City Council voted last year to raise its minimum wage to $15 an hour, making it the highest in the nation. At the national level, President Barack Obama took executive action to raise the minimum wage to $10.10 for federal contract workers; similar legislation to raise the federal minimum wage for all Americans has stalled in Congress. APHA has shown support for raising the minimum wage, including advocacy on a Senate bill last year that would have increased it nationally. The issue is expected to come up again in Congress.

For a growing chorus of public health practitioners, raising the minimum wage is a fundamental step in addressing two key determinants of health: income and poverty.

"Income affects everything," said Rajiv Bhatia, MD, MPH, founder and director of the Civic Engine, a consulting group focused on health and sustainability. "Income may not be the strongest risk factor for any particular disease or outcome, but it's a risk factor for all of them."

Bhatia previously worked at the San Francisco Department of Public Health, where he led an assessment on the health benefits of a local living wage ordinance that would raise the hourly wage to $11. The study, which was published in 2001 in APHA's *American Journal of Public Health*, found that the wage increase would decrease the risk of premature death by 5 percent for adults ages 24 to 44 living in households with an income of about $20,000. In addition, the children of such workers would experience substantially increased odds of high school completion and a 22 percent decrease in the risk of early childbirth.

More recently, Bhatia authored a 2014 report for Human Impact Partners on a legislative proposal to raise California's minimum wage to $13 by 2017. That report, "Health Impacts of Raising California's Minimum Wage," found that the wage increase would prevent nearly 400 premature deaths among lower-income Californians each year. The report also noted that nationwide, people with incomes above the federal poverty line typically live more than five years longer than those below the poverty line. Bhatia noted that growing public outcry to raise wages for those at the bottom of the economic ladder presents public health practitioners with the perfect opportunity to speak out.

"When the public is calling for something, you have a safe path to get behind it," he told *The Nation's Health.* "I think this is an interesting test for public health."

Indeed, a number of local minimum wage campaigns have attracted the support of health organizations. In Illinois, the AIDS Foundation of Chicago is a coalition member of Raise Illinois, a campaign to increase the state minimum wage to $10.65. According to Suraj Madoori, MPH, MSJ, MA, manager of the foundation's HIV Prevention Justice Alliance, supporting the campaign was a natural fit, as the research shows that "poverty and HIV go hand in hand--HIV is becoming a disease of poverty in many ways, especially in communities of color.

"You can raise your health status and lower your risk for so many other conditions because you don't face the psychological stress of trying to find housing or making sure your family can eat," he said. "By having the ability to get out of poverty, you can really think beyond those basic needs."

To the west in Oakland, California, the Street Level Health Project joined the steering committee of Lift Up Oakland, which campaigned in support of a successful 2014 ballot measure that raised the minimum wage to $12.25. Joel Aguiar, interim executive director of the Street Level Health Project, which provides health and social services to underserved immigrant communities, said the additional income will have a "huge effect" on the ability of low-wage immigrant workers to care for their health. "It'll mean someone who might not have been able to pay rent one month will not become homeless," Aguiar said. "This isn't just a workers' rights issue--this is a public health issue."

Unfortunately, minimum wage campaigns rarely go unopposed, with opponents arguing that wage increases are bad for business. However, the U.S. Department of Labor cites research finding that minimum wage increases have no "discernable effect" on employment, and that most small business owners believe higher wages are offset by decreased employee turnover and increased consumer spending power. In fact, research is finding that higher wages also benefit state health care spending.

In an October 2014 report from the Center for American Progress, "A Win-Win for Working Families and State Budgets: Pairing Medicaid Expansion and a $10.10 Minimum Wage," authors found that higher minimum wages reduce enrollment in traditional Medicaid--the portion of the health insurance program in which states pay a substantial share.

Combined with an expansion in Medicaid eligibility, which was authorized via the Affordable Care Act and funded via federal dollars, a $10.10 minimum wage would reduce states' pre-health reform Medicaid spending by more than $2.5 billion each year, the report found.

"The public health community may not feel like it has a set of tools to advocate for policies that raise wages," said report coauthor Rachel West, MPP, senior policy analyst with the Poverty to Prosperity Program at the Center for American Progress. "But with Medicaid expansion--this is one policy that directly addresses economic challenges and builds a bridge to health care access."

For APHA member Rex Archer, MD, MPH, director of health for the Kansas City, Missouri, Health Department, achieving a "living wage has become one of the most important public health issues for us, period." According to Archer, 47 percent of annual deaths in Kansas City are attributable to six root social factors, including individual- and community-level poverty and income inequality. In fact, average life expectancy varies by more than 10 years across Kansas City ZIP codes, with those at the bottom rung characterized by much higher rates of poverty and much lower family incomes.

"We can't treat our way out of this problem," he said. "We can't ignore the stress of not having a living wage and what that's doing to our population."

1. How and why is the public health community advocating for higher minimum wages? Are their arguments convincing?

2. If you opposed minimum wage increases, how might you counter the claim that an increase in the minimum wage is an important public health issue?

"THE IMPLICATIONS OF INCOME INEQUALITY," BY WILL KRAMER, FROM *RISK MANAGEMENT*, NOVEMBER 2, 2015

NIGEL TRAVIS IS THE CHAIRMAN AND CEO OF DUNKIN' BRANDS, THE PARENT COMPANY OF DUNKIN' DONUTS AND Baskin Robbins. And as of his July appearance on CNNMoney, where he commented on the news that New York's Wage Board recommended that fast food workers earn $15 per hour, he is also an internet meme. A picture of Travis has circulated on social media with the caption, 'Dunkin Donuts' CEO says $15 an hour is 'outrageous.' He makes $4,889 an hour."

Several articles in major newspapers have also criticized Travis with headlines like "Dunkin' Donuts CEO tone deaf on minimum wage" in The Boston Globe and "Dunkin' CEO says raising minimum wage to $15-per-hour is 'absolutely outrageous'...as he lives in mansion and makes $10 million per year" in the Daily Mail. Seattle Times columnist Jon Talton went so far as to call Travis "the best advocate for the $15 minimum wage," writing that "when high-paid executives get hysterical about improving the pay of their workers, it doesn't help their case."

Nigel Travis is not the first corporate leader to be targeted by advocacy groups and the media for a compensation package that dwarfs those of the company's workers, and he certainly won't be the last. In August, the Securities and Exchange Commission adopted a final rule that will require every public company to disclose the ratio of their CEO's total compensation compared to that of the organization's median worker. Although the rule does not go into effect until the fiscal year beginning Jan. 1, 2017, its adoption has already drawn concern throughout the business community. Considering the uproar stemming from Travis' brief commentary on a proposed minimum wage increase, corporate leaders must assess all of the risks that can stem from the increasing focus on income inequality.

THE CONTEXT OF INCOME INEQUALITY

WHILE THE United States has always been an

economically unequal society, most economists agree that inequality has been increasing since the 1970s. According to the Economic Policy Institute, a nonprofit and nonpartisan think tank, the CEO-to-worker compensation ratio was 20:1 in 1965 and grew steadily to almost 196:1 in 2013. Meanwhile, Emmanuel Saez and Gabriel Zucman, economic researchers at the University of California, Berkeley, found that the share of all wealth owned by the richest 0.1% of Americans has grown from 7% in 1978 to 22% in 2012.

Until recently, many Americans seemed not to know or care about the growing divide in income and wealth. Even at the height of the so-called Great Recession in 2009, only 47% of Americans polled by Pew Research agreed that there were "very strong" or "strong" conflicts between the nations rich and the poor. By late 2011, that figure had grown to 66%. Since then, income inequality has become a regular topic of political debate and public discourse.

Many observers attribute the increasing focus on wealth and economic inequality to the Occupy Wall Street movement that began in New York City's Zuccotti Park in September 2011 and spread to cities and towns across the country. Although the protestors were derided at the time for not outlining a clear platform of demands, their efforts to provoke public discussion about income inequality and the divide between the 99% and the 1% has had a lasting impact.

Less than a year later, in November 2012, approximately 200 fast food workers in New York went on strike, demanding a $15 minimum wage in what was then the largest labor action in the industry. The "Fight for 15" movement grew from there, holding strikes and walk-outs, filing lawsuits over wage theft, and generally keeping the issue of income inequality prominent in the media. On April 15, 2015, roughly 60,000 workers in more than 200 cities across the United States took part in the largest coordinated protest by low-wage workers in history. By then, the movement had grown beyond the fast food industry to include home-care workers, child-care staff, security guards and anyone who earned less than what they considered to be a living wage.

As of mid-2015, Seattle, San Francisco and Los Angeles have begun phasing in a $15 minimum wage. Democratic presidential candidate Sen. Bernie Sanders introduced Congressional legislation to raise the federal minimum wage to $15 per hour. What was once considered inconceivable has become more and more commonly accepted as a necessary and even moral imperative for many American businesses.

THE RISKS OF THE PAY RATIO DISCLOSURE RULE

A RECENT online presentation by business law firm Dorsey & Whitney LLP and Cam Hoang, senior counsel and assistant corporate secretary at General Mills, examined many of the risks public companies face as a result of the SEC's new pay ratio disclosure rule. At the most obvious level, Dorsey & Whitney predicts that companies with high ratios between CEO and median worker pay may see negative consequences related to media coverage and public relations. The compensation for the CEOs of public companies is already disclosed in SEC filings, and such disclosures have led to negative attention for companies with highly-compensated executives. For example, the AFL-CIO reports that one of the most highly-trafficked sections of its website it its Executive PayWatch page, which names the 100 most highly-compensated CEOs in America alongside testimonials from low-wage workers at their companies. Similarly, California-based nonprofit As You Sow recently published a report entitled The 100 Most Overpaid CEOs: Executive Compensation at S&P 500 Companies. Apart from potentially influencing public opinion, the AFL-CIO, As You Sow and like-minded organizations also lobby institutional investors, such as mutual and pension funds, to closely examine executive compensation data for their stock holdings as a measure of shareholder value. This attention will only increase as information about the relative compensation of public companies' median employees becomes public.

Beyond the public relations implications, Dorsey & Whitney also noted potential employee-related issues for firms with low median employee pay, such as reduced morale and a negative impact on hiring and retention. While pay is often a taboo subject among co-workers, disclosing the median compensation for workers at any firm will inevitability lead employees to compare them-selves against that measure. Particularly for those who fall below the median, this information may hurt morale and productivity, and even lead some to seek employment elsewhere if they feel the median compensation is too low to justify putting more time and effort toward moving up in the organization. Conversely, morale may be boosted among those employees who are paid above the median thanks to their improved understanding of their value within the organization.

Finally, it remains an open question how the public will be affected by this information. In a recent working paper, Harvard Business School researchers Bhavya Mohan, Michael Norton and Rohit Deshpande found in six separate studies that pay ratio disclosure can indeed affect the intentions of consumers. Given an informed choice, they found consumers would prefer to purchase from firms with relatively low CEO-to-median-worker pay ratio such as 5:1 or even 60:1, as opposed to firms with high ratios such as 1000:1. Lower CEO-to-median-worker pay ratios also improved consumer perceptions of products at different price points as well as their ratings of the firm's warmth and competence. Further, the researchers found that firms with a high CEO-to-median-worker pay ratio must offer a 50% price discount to achieve the same customer satisfaction that a firm with a low ratio achieves at full price.

From negative publicity to reduced investor stock valuation, and from reduced employee morale to diminished customer opinion, it appears that the increased social focus on income inequality from the SEC's pay ratio rule may have significant potential risk management implications for public companies.

MITIGATING PAY RATIO DISCLOSURE RISKS

GIVEN THAT the ever-increasing disparity between executive and worker pay is such a widespread phenomenon, risk managers at individual companies might be at a loss to imagine what they alone can do to address the issue. Fortunately, experts in the field have already begun to weigh in.

Eleanor Bloxham, founder and CEO of The Value Alliance, an advisory firm for multinational public companies and private start-ups, provided a comment letter to the SEC supporting the pay ratio disclosure rule as an important development for both investors and companies. She acknowledged the risks of the new rule for public companies, but also suggested its implementation could be an opportunity for corporate leaders to reexamine their compensation strategies for the long-term benefit of their employees and shareholders.

Because the SEC rule requires the calculation of total compensation including benefits, Bloxham suggested that companies could increase employee stock ownership as a method to boost the compensation of the median worker. Even more important, she said, corporate leaders need to begin to understand how their employees actually live in order to better inform decision-making about compensation.

One unconventional way to increase this understanding would be to take a note from the Undercover Boss television show where executives work alongside low-level employees, Bloxham said. In her experience, too many companies have gotten away from the age-old strategy of "management by walking around." Crucially, she noted, "communication at the workers [regarding compensation] is not going to get anywhere. Instead, we need communications that begin with understanding and learning from the workers, and with the workers."

For a company with a higher CEO-to-median-worker compensation ratio, there is no easy answer to how it will mitigate the risks to its reputation, stock value, employee morale and customer opinion. One thing risk managers can agree upon is that the time to begin addressing these issues is now, rather than in 2017.

THE BROADER IMPLICATIONS FOR ALL ORGANIZATIONS

PERHAPS THE greatest risk to American organizations regarding income inequality is the greatest unknown: How far will the public take its concern? What began as the rallying cry of an encampment of disenfranchised people in New York City has gone on to propel one of the largest labor movements in recent memory and has imbedded itself into the consciousness of Americans of all races, classes and creeds. The unfairness of the current economic system is no longer just a discussion topic in universities and coffee shops, but in factories and on the streets of every American city.

While the SEC's pay ratio rule only directly impacts public companies, privately-held organizations should consider the likelihood that their stakeholders and customers may begin asking for this information as well. As the Fight for 15 movement continues to have success, employers offering less to their workers may rightly wonder how that decision will affect their reputation in their communities and among their own employees.

All indications are that discussions around income inequality and specific proposals such as the $15 minimum wage will only increase as the 2016 election season ramps up. Corporate leaders must therefore begin intentionally addressing the related risks, or risk joining Dunkin' Brands' Nigel Travis in the world of internet infamy.

1. Do you think companies with high CEO to median worker pay ratios will heed this article's advice?

2. Chipotle Mexican Grill has a CEO to median pay ratio of over 1000:1. Yet the company has also taken innovative steps unusual in the industry such as removing GMO foods from their menu. Does this point to any potentially positive incentives for companies to attract competent leadership through high (even if unfair) compensation?

CHAPTER 5

WHAT THE MEDIA SAY

As we know, economic data on the effects of a minimum wage increase are inconclusive. In a situation open to interpretation, one might expect the media to play a decisive role in shaping public opinion either for or against increases in the minimum wage. This would be a correct assumption to make. Although in Chapter Six we'll see that most Americans support a higher minimum wage, many mainstream media outlets continue to parrot the now-familiar arguments against a higher minimum wage: it will harm those at the bottom rung of society most, it will cause unemployment, and it will weaken economic growth.

This chapter begins with a critique of the many newspapers and magazines arguing against minimum wage increases. Ironically, as Aaron Pacitti and Mike Cauvel write in the first selection, many journalists choose not to fairly represent the benefits of minimum wage increases out of a fear of appearing "biased." Other journalists might be fearful of siding with workers instead of the large media conglomerations that employ them.

Media bias also surfaces through selective reporting. The nationwide "Fight for $15" and fast-food strikes receive sporadic coverage. Of course, with a presidential election, a massive refugee crisis, to say nothing of mass shootings and terror attacks preoccupying the nation, it's little wonder that traditional "old-school" class and labor issues have receded to the background of media analysis. Nonetheless, as the businesses owners profiled in our final piece about Portland, Maine's new wage initiative attest, attempts to balance economic survival with just compensation for workers will persist. For those paying attention, the outcomes are harbingers of what working Americans can expect moving into the next decade.

"WHY WON'T THE MEDIA ADMIT THAT NEW YORK'S NEW MINIMUM WAGE POLICY WILL BE GOOD FOR BUSINESS?" BY AARON PACITTI, FROM THE *HUFFINGTON POST,* AUGUST 4, 2015

CO-AUTHORED BY MIKE CAUVEL, Ph.D. CANDIDATE IN ECONOMICS AT AMERICAN UNIVERSITY

Last week the New York State Fast Food Wage Board approved a measure that will increase the minimum wage for fast food workers to $15 per hour by 2021. Many proponents, such as Governor Andrew Cuomo, have supported this policy by invoking notions of economic justice. Although this is certainly a step towards a more just economy, which is reason enough to enact such a policy, focusing only on this aspect of the reform actually undersells the benefits to workers and businesses of increasing wages.

Research shows that raising the minimum wage has a number of economic benefits. It puts more money in the pockets of those who will actually spend it, leading to higher sales, and increases efficiency by reducing worker turnover and incentivizing employees to be more productive, lowering business costs.

The benefits could be stronger if the minimum wage hike was applied statewide, and not just for those at large franchises in one industry -- firms that are large and profitable enough to absorb the increased costs without engaging in layoffs. Even without state- and industry-wide legislation, many low-wage workers will see substantial benefits from this policy, as a higher minimum wage for fast food workers will likely have ripple effects that increase wages for a large number of workers in lower income brackets.

Though some advocates have noted economic arguments in favor of raising the minimum wage, most have focused on questions of fairness. This is evident, for example, in Governor Cuomo's rhetoric about lifting these workers and their families out of poverty, and his argument that full-time workers should not have to rely upon public assistance. While these arguments are certainly compelling, this strategy has led to a distorted view of this policy, with debate seemingly focused on a nonexistent tradeoff between the wellbeing of a small subset of struggling workers and the health of the economy.

The media has shaped this misperception by essentially ignoring any discussion of the policy's positive economic implications. Instead, it has almost exclusively discussed the possible, but unlikely, downsides, relaying the views of CEOs and business owners, who have reacted unsurprisingly by claiming that it will ultimately hurt workers.

The CEO of Dunkin' Donuts, Nigel Travis, grabbed headlines by calling the $15 an hour minimum wage "outrageous," even though he will still make about as much in a single day as a full-time worker would earn in a year at this wage rate. Although he stopped short of threatening to fire employees, perhaps learning from the missteps of CEOs who made similar remarks regarding the Affordable Care Act, he did claim that his firm would likely hire fewer workers and that the rise in wages would lead to job losses. Mr. Travis, and the media, simply ignore the ways that companies like Dunkin' Donuts would benefit in the long run, offsetting most of the higher labor costs.

This is hardly an isolated incident. CEOs and business owners often respond to even the slightest hint that policies may lead to increased benefits for workers, such as the election of a Democratic president, by threatening to punish employees -- a malicious, childish, and borderline criminal approach. Though these threats have often backfired or never materialized, they are still a nearly automatic response for business leaders.

So why have discussions of the policy's economic consequences in the media been so one-sided? Ironically, it is because journalists don't want to appear biased and engage in "shape-of-planet-differ" reporting, giving equal weight to both sides of the issue and limiting discussion of the benefits, even though there is no evidence that increases in the minimum wage lead to net job losses.

Although small businesses, which operate with thinner profit margins, might adjust to a higher minimum wage by engaging in layoffs or hours reductions, there are a number of policy options that could reduce the burden on these businesses. Furthermore, other, larger, firms -- like those in the fast food industry -- could hire more workers due to the positive effects on sales, productivity, and turn-over. Thus, at the firm level there might be instances of job losses in some sectors and job gains in others. But at the state-wide macro level, there would be no negative net effect or a small positive net effect on employment.

The reason labor can violate the law of demand is that businesses can offset higher labor costs in several ways that don't involve layoffs. The first is price increases. But estimates suggest that a minimum wage of $15 per hour would only lead to a 4 percent hike in prices, raising the cost of a cup of coffee at Dunkin' Donuts from around $2 to $2.08.

Higher labor costs could also be covered by decreases in profits or dividend payouts for fast food corporations, which is likely why they are so vehe-mently opposed to this policy. In fact, supporters of a higher minimum wage have frequently cited the massive profits of fast food corporations, and this is probably the reason that the new wages would only affect franchises with more than 30 locations nationwide. However, the effects on prices and profits are likely to be minor because increased costs will be offset by increased productivity due to greater effort, lower turnover (which can save employers $4,700 per employee), and higher sales. Furthermore, the wage hikes will be spread out over the course of several years to prevent large shocks to firms.

If corporations could save money by employing fewer workers, they would have cut payrolls long ago. Of course, raising wages does affect the calculus of hiring workers, hours, benefits, and buying machines, and some have argued that it will lead to greater automation in affected industries. However, automation began prior to any increases in the minimum wage, and it will ultimately be up to consumers to decide whether automated kiosks are adequate substitutes for human customer service employees.

In an economy where corporate profits are at record highs while average wages have stagnated for decades, we don't have to choose between economic justice and common economic sense. It is possible to improve living standards for full-time, low-income workers without bringing business to its knees. The media shouldn't pretend otherwise.

1. Does this author appear to be cherry-picking his facts, or presenting a balanced view?

2. What are some other reasons why the fast food industry might feel insecure about its long-term sustainability and profitability?

"BALLOT QUESTION RAISING MINIMUM WAGE TO $15 WILL AFFECT MORE THAN PORTLAND," BY EDWARD D. MURPHY, FROM THE *PORTLAND PRESS HERALD*, OCTOBER 18, 2015

ADVOCATES SAY THE MEASURE IS NEEDED TO ADDRESS RISING LIVING COSTS, WHILE OPPONENTS SAY IT WILL FORCE BUSINESSES TO SHRINK STAFF OR MOVE OUT.

Members of Portland's Green Independent Committee watched officials struggle with a plan to raise the city's minimum wage this year and concluded it had a basic flaw: It was far too timid.

With other cities around the country -- Seattle, San Francisco and Los Angeles among them -- raising the minimum hourly pay to $15, Portland was settling too low by backing $10.10 an hour, said Mako Bates, one of the Green activists who believes that basic fairness requires a more dramatic increase.

But the Greens' proposal for a $15-an-hour minimum wage, which will be on the ballot Nov. 3, would essentially double the statewide minimum wage and dramatically hike the City Council-adopted minimum that will take effect in January. It has touched off strong opposition from the business community and stoked fears that businesses could slow hiring or lay off workers, relocate outside of Portland or even fold up altogether. It also presents a complicated set of legal and enforcement issues that bewilder and alarm employers, from small retailers to large nonprofits.

Backers, on the other hand, say businesses need to be forced to increase pay for a range of reasons, including income inequality, the high cost of living in Portland and a minimum wage that has remained stuck, since 2009, at $7.50 an hour in Maine.

The opponents are making the most noise in the campaign so far, rallying around a slogan that says the increase would be "Too Far, Too Fast."

Chris Hall, chief executive officer of the Portland Regional Chamber of Commerce, said there's a big difference between the economies and wage scales in Portland and $15-an-hour cities such as Seattle and San Francisco, where the business communities have larger and faster-growing high-tech firms. According to the federal Bureau of Labor Statistics, the metro area of Seattle has a mean annual wage of $59,130 and San Francisco has $64,990 compared with Portland's $42,140.

Portland has smaller companies and the economy remains fragile, even six years after the recession, Hall said.

"In Portland, you're really pushing the envelope when you get to $15," Hall said. "People are really worried that they may not be able to continue their businesses."

WORRIES OVER ATTRACTING WORKERS

Bates said he's heard that argument before and attributes some of it to hyperbole and some to business owners not understanding that wages would increase gradually to $15. For small businesses, the full $15 wouldn't go into effect until July 1, 2019. For bigger businesses, which are defined as companies that employ more than 500 workers nationally, minimum hourly wages would rise to $12 next July 1 and then to $15 on July 1, 2017.

"We wanted it to be something that would actually work for people living in the city," Bates said, while the phase-in schedule is intended to reduce the shock on businesses.

Lower-wage workers "work in a city and they can't afford to live there," Bates said, a situation that he said isn't helped by either the current state minimum wage of $7.50 an hour or the $10.10 minimum in Portland that will kick in on Jan. 1. According to the online realty company Zillow, rents in the city rose 17 percent from May 2014 to May of this year.

Bates reasons that if the federal minimum had risen at the rate of inflation since the last time it was increased more than six years ago, it likely would be more than $11 an hour -- although according to the Bureau of Labor Statistics, inflation has been so low since 2009 that the amount would be $8.33 an hour, adjusted for increases in the consumer price index.

If you factored in increases in worker productivity, Bates argued, the minimum should be more than $20 an hour.

Opponents, however, say that the city's businesses will be put in a difficult position if they have to pay workers double what their competitors are paying people doing the same job in a neighboring town.

For Ellis Baum, it would make attracting workers far more difficult. Baum is the regional director for Residential Resources, which runs group homes for developmentally disabled adults. The company operates a group home in Portland and serves two clients in another Portland home. He said the company has a staff of about 120 in the homes it operates in Maine, providing a range of services from preparing meals to helping with dressing and hygiene. In all, the company serves about 35 clients in group homes, he said, and another 20 or so who are in foster homes.

Baum said a tightening labor market already makes it difficult for the company to attract employees even though it pays about $10 per hour -- well over the current minimum wage of $7.50. It's not unusual for workers to leave for a 25-cent-an-hour increase, he said. If $15 per hour becomes the new minimum wage in Portland -- a 50 percent increase over what he pays now -- he fears he won't be able to keep workers in Portland who will go to less-demanding jobs.

"I don't know where I would get staff," Baum said. "Someone could work at McDonald's or Starbucks, with a very low responsibility position and make more than what I'm offering now."

In general, the company is reimbursed at about $16 an hour by the state, so an increase in workers' pay to $15 a hour in its Portland operations would eliminate almost all the company money for overhead, administration and profits.

Even with wages at about $10 an hour, Baum said, the company had losses in July and August because of training costs for the new workers it brought on because of high turnover.

With the added costs in wages, Baum said, the company would have to consider dropping its Portland clients and would likely face the need to pay its workers more for other positions in Maine. The company pays 80 percent of its workers' health insurance costs and that could be imperiled if pay rates have to be boosted, he said.

BANGING THE POLITICAL DRUMS

The campaign itself is shaping up as a bit of a mismatch, at least in terms of spending. Hall, whose chamber is helping to spearhead the "Too Far, Too Fast" opposition to the proposal, said he expects the group will need to spend about $100,000. In the group's initial finance report, filed with the city Oct. 1, the political action committee had raised $3,150 and spent $11,750 for legal costs and website design.

By way of comparison, the two main groups involved in a Portland referendum last June to block the sale of Congress Square plaza to an adjacent hotel spent nearly $70,000 combined.

Bates said there's no way proponents could raise anywhere near as much as the opponents plan to for the referendum campaign.

He said the supporters' biggest expenditure is likely to be yard signs, and backers will also mobilize teams to go door to door explaining the need for a higher minimum wage.

The Maine People's Alliance -- which is gathering signatures for a 2016 ballot initiative to raise the statewide minimum wage to $12 -- conducted a poll in late summer that indicated 48.2 percent of Portland voters backed the increase and 39.7 percent opposed it. The other 12.1 percent hadn't decided.

Not surprisingly, however, business owners were opposed in a survey conducted in late September by Portland Buy Local.

The survey of 100 local business owners found 63 oppose the $15-an-hour referendum, but 66 back the council's new minimum wage.

The survey also found that the majority of the businesses -- 56 -- pay their workers between $9 an hour and $14.99 an hour.

Kirk Dyson, who works at the Nickelodeon Theater in downtown Portland and also at the Portland Radio Group, said he makes less than $15 an hour at both jobs.

But even though it would mean a raise, he's not sure a hike in the minimum wage to $15 is a good idea.

"I feel like $15 is a little high, to be honest," he said, although he added, "I feel that in places like New York, that makes sense."

Dyson said he worries that if the minimum is increased to $15, employers will stop hiring. But he said the $10.10 wage the council has adopted is more palatable and probably wouldn't hurt employment prospects.

Travis Horner, a hair-cutting specialist at J. Henry Salon on Free Street, said his employer has already started cutting hours to prepare for the minimum wage hike coming in January. Horner said he worries that more reductions would follow if the referendum passes.

New hires at the salon are paid minimum wage for a year while they learn the craft, Horner said, but then switch to commission-based compensation. If those who are on commission don't make enough to match the minimum wage, the salon has to make up the difference, he said.

Horner said the salon is relatively new and "on the profitable/non-profitable line" and he worries that higher labor costs could make it difficult for the salon to survive.

LEGAL KNOTS, AND LIKELY CHALLENGES

If the ballot measure is approved, some wrinkles in the new law would have to be ironed out before it goes into effect a month after Election Day. And there are likely to be legal challenges.

For instance, the minimum wage law would apply not only to Portland employers and employees, but also to companies that are based outside of Portland and send employees to work in Portland. If a company is based outside of Portland, it would have to pay $15 to hourly workers while they are working inside the city. Portland-based companies would also need to pay $15 an hour for a worker who's sent outside the city, as long as that employee "primarily or substantially" works inside the city limits.

That language adds uncertainty to the law, said David Webbert of the law firm Johnson, Webbert & Young, which specializes in employment issues. He said "primarily" has been defined as 50 percent-plus. But "substantially" is less clear, Webbert said, so opponents may turn to the courts for a definition.

And enforcing the wage laws, which normally falls on the Maine Department of Labor, would now be a task given to the city manager, under both the City Council's wage plan and the referendum. City spokeswoman Jessica Grondin said the city isn't planning to hire a wage investigator, although that could change if there are widespread allegations that employers aren't paying their workers properly.

The law would also have a big impact on restaurants and tipped workers, a subject that tied up the council when it tackled the city's minimum wage law over the summer.

Currently, tipped workers earn a minimum of $3.75 an hour from their employer, with the rest of their $7.50 hourly wage to come from tips. If the workers don't earn enough in tips to reach minimum wage, the restaurant has to make up the difference.

In initially adopting the $10.10 minimum wage, the council doubled the base wage that restaurants had to pay servers, but then rolled it back -- employers will still have to make up the difference if servers don't make enough in tips to earn $10.10 an hour.

The ballot proposal would raise the amount employers would have to pay servers to $11.25 an hour and make them responsible for the difference between that and $15 an hour if tips don't cover the gap.

Steve DiMillo, whose family owns DiMillo's on the Water, said that could force him and other restaurant owners to change the way they operate, possibly going to a more casual dining atmosphere in order to hire fewer servers. Others have said they may raise prices to cover higher wages and discourage tipping as a way to offset the higher prices. Still others are considering using technology so that tablets and table-mounted monitors receive patrons' orders directly, reducing the need for wait staff.

SOME UNLIKELY OPPONENTS

The size of the increase has brought out unlikely opponents, including Jim Wellehan, the owner of Lamey-Wellehan Shoe Stores, and one of the first signers of a Maine People's Alliance effort to get a statewide minimum wage increase on the ballot next fall.

That statewide measure would raise the minimum wage in annual steps, culminating with a $12-an-hour minimum in 2020.

Wellehan said many of his workers already earn $15 an hour, but that wage is built on incentives for taking classes, like one called "retail pedorthics," which trains salespeople to help customers with foot problems. He said his goal is to make his shoe stores more of a full-service stop for people looking not only for shoes, but help with foot problems. Starting everyone at $15 an hour would give workers little reason to take extra classes, Wellehan said, as well as create headaches for business owners who have some workers in Portland and others outside the city.

But Wellehan said that his opposition to a $15-an-hour minimum doesn't blind him to the need for change in pay scales and to address income inequality.

"I would love to have a $20 minimum wage around the world," he said. "We need a minimum wage that's higher and a maximum wage that's lower."

1. Do you think a fifteen-dollar-per-hour minimum wage is too high in a small city such as Portland, Maine?

2. What other positive benefits could arise from higher wages, both for workers and employers?

CHAPTER 6

WHAT ORDINARY PEOPLE SAY

A sizeable, if not overwhelming, majority of Americans favor policies aimed at reducing income inequality. Increasing the minimum wage is perhaps the most legible and visible of these policies. But do the net benefits outweigh the net costs? Again, the answer appears to depend on whom you ask.

Thanks to movements such as Occupy Wall Street, the 2008 financial downturn sparked a marked increase in concern with widening income inequality among average citizens. President Obama echoed these sentiments, defining the amelioration of both inequality and diminished economic prospects as "the defining challenge of our time." Eighty-five percent of the Democratic Party, and surprisingly, almost half of an increasingly right-leaning Republican Party support this basic position. But disagreement about how best to achieve this popular goal has caused experimentation to lag. Consequently, inequality continues to get worse.

Although politicians and ordinary citizens agree that full-time work should provide a living wage, a powerful business lobby buttressed by biased economists stand in the way of easy victory. Moreover, small employers often line up against wage increases as well. These firms tend to worry about their own survival and bottom line, and downplay abstract questions of equality and economic justice.

While Americans are at least superficially wary of growing inequality, decades of union-bashing, deregulation and free-market ideology, and an ingrained distrust of any overtly redistributive policy promise an uphill battle to raise the minimum wage, despite popular and political support.

"MAJORITY OF AMERICANS WANT MINIMUM WAGE TO BE INCREASED, POLL FINDS," BY MICHAEL A. FLETCHER AND PEYTON M. CRAIGHILL, FROM THE *WASHINGTON POST*, DECEMBER 18, 2013

A large majority of Americans want Congress to substantially increase the minimum wage as part of an effort to reduce the nation's expanding economic inequality, according to a new Washington Post-ABC News poll.

As a growing share of the country's income flows

to the very wealthiest, the poll found that 57 percent of Americans say lawmakers should pursue policies aimed at balancing an economic system they think is out of whack. Nearly two in three say federal policy is tilted toward helping the rich over Americans who are less well-off, according to the survey.

The findings come as President Obama has moved to refocus national attention on the problems of inequality and decreasing social mobility. Earlier this month, he called confronting the twin issues "the defining challenge of our time." He added that "making sure our economy works for every working American" will be a central task of his remaining time in office.

Obama recently came out in favor of raising the minimum wage to $10.10 an hour — a much larger increase than he had proposed in his State of the Union address in February, when he advocated raising it to $9 an hour.

Increasing the minimum wage, which has stood at $7.25 an hour since 2009, is one of the chief policy tools economists recommend to address inequality. It is also popular among everyday Americans: About two in three say the wage floor should be lifted, and the average wage suggested is $9.41 an hour.

The idea of using public policy to combat inequality is much more popular among Democrats and independents than it is among Republicans. Three in four Democrats and 58 percent of independents say Washington should pursue policies to address inequality, a sentiment that was shared by just two in five Republicans.

A similar divide is evident when it comes to the minimum wage. Eighty-five percent of Democrats support raising the wage, while Republicans are split 50-45 on the issue, the poll found. Republicans support a lower wage floor than Democrats, when asked separately about their preferred dollar amount. On average, Democrats favor a minimum wage of just over $10, while Republicans want it to be about $8.60 an hour. Independents fall in between, supporting an average minimum wage of about $9.40 an hour. All three groups set their preferred minimum wage higher than the current $7.25, but far below a $15 wage sought by some worker advocates.

Although partisans disagree about what should be done about inequality, economists say the issue has reached dimensions not seen since the years preceding the Great Depression.

Whether calculated by comparing the growth in wages of the highest-income Americans with the lowest, or the proportion of wealth controlled by the richest Americans, or the ratio of wages for production workers to those of chief executives, inequality has grown. Americans have consistently called for government to aim policies at shrinking the gap.

Two years ago, when the Occupy Wall Street movement helped move the issue into the mainstream of political debate, a Post-ABC poll found that more than six in 10 perceived a widening wealth gap and 60 percent wanted Washington to pursue policy to address it, similar to today's 57 percent mark. In the fall of 2012, 52 percent of registered voters shared that sentiment.

Although some policymakers point to minimum-wage increases, more widespread unionization, better education opportunities and bolstering income-support programs such as the Earned Income Tax Credit as possible remedies, enacting those policies has always proved difficult.

"A majority of the public might favor some policies that the minority that has the most influence is less enthusiastic about," said Martin Gilens, a politics professor at Princeton University. "On some policies, there is ambivalence among the public. While there is strong support for opportunity-enhancing policies to reduce inequality, there is less support for directly redistributive policies."

Obama has periodically invoked inequality as a problem and promised to address it. Yet economic inequality has only widened on his watch.

Between 2009 and 2012, the incomes of the top 1 percent of earners grew by more than 31 percent, according to Emmanuel Saez, an economist at the University of California at Berkeley, while the incomes of the bottom 99 percent expanded by just 0.4 percent. "He's got a Republican House and even members of the Democratic Party who are strongly aligned with business interest, who are at best ambivalent about some of these policies that certainly are not popular among business interests that have to foot the bill," Gilens said. "When you have divided government and multiple veto points, policies that even a majority of people support can be difficult to adopt."

The new Post-ABC poll was conducted Dec. 12-15 among a random national sample of 1,005 adults, including interviews on land lines and with cellphone-only respondents. The overall margin of sampling error is plus or minus 3.5 percentage points.

Scott Clement contributed to this report.

1. Do you think increasing the minimum wage is the best tool to counter inequality? Why or why not? What are some alternatives?

2. Why do you think most Americans view income inequality as a problem, but oppose any redistributive policies? If you were in charge of "selling" such a policy, how might you repackage it?

"NICKEL AND DIMED IN 2016: YOU CAN'T EARN A LIVING ON THE MINIMUM WAGE," BY PETER VAN BUREN, FROM TOMDISPATCH.COM, FEBRUARY 16 2016

When presidential candidate Bernie Sanders talks about income inequality, and when other candidates speak about the minimum wage and food stamps, what are they really talking about?

Whether they know it or not, it's something like this.

MY WORKING LIFE THEN

A few years ago, I wrote about my experience enmeshed in the minimum-wage economy, chronicling the collapse of good people who could not earn enough money, often working 60-plus hours a week at multiple jobs, to feed their families. I saw that, in this country, people trying to make ends meet in such a fashion still had to resort to food benefit programs and charity. I saw an employee fired for stealing lunches from the break room refrigerator to feed himself. I watched as a co-worker secretly brought her two kids into the store and left them to wander alone for hours because she couldn't afford childcare. (As it happens, 29% of low-wage employees are single parents.)

At that point, having worked at the State Department for 24 years, I had been booted out for being a whistleblower. I wasn't sure what would happen to me next and so took a series of minimum wage jobs. Finding myself plunged into the low-wage economy was a sobering, even frightening, experience that made me realize just how ignorant I had been about the lives of the people who rang me up at stores or served me food in restaurants. Though millions of adults work for minimum wage, until I did it myself I knew nothing about what that involved, which meant I knew next to nothing about twenty-first-century America.

I was lucky. I didn't become one of those millions of people trapped as the "working poor." I made it out. But with all the election talk about the economy, I decided it was time to go back and take another look at where I had been, and where too many others still are.

MY WORKING LIFE NOW

I found things were pretty much the same in 2016 as they were in 2012, which meant -- because there was no real improvement -- that things were actually worse.

This time around, I worked for a month and a half at a national retail chain in New York City. While mine was hardly a scientific experiment, I'd be willing to bet an hour of my minimum-wage salary ($9 before taxes) that what follows is pretty typical of the New Economy.

Just getting hired wasn't easy for this 56-year-old guy. To become a sales clerk, peddling items that were generally well under $50 a pop, I needed two previous employment references and I had to pass a credit check. Unlike some low-wage jobs, a mandatory drug test wasn't part of the process, but there was a criminal background check and I was told drug offenses would disqualify me. I was given an exam twice, by two different managers, designed to see how I'd respond to various customer situations. In other words, anyone without some education, good English, a decent work history, and a clean record wouldn't even qualify for minimum-wage money at this chain.

And believe me, I earned that money. Any shift under six hours involved only a 15-minute break (which cost the company just $2.25). Trust me, at my age, after hours standing, I needed that break and I wasn't even the oldest or least fit employee. After six hours, you did get a 45-minute break, but were only paid for 15 minutes of it.

The hardest part of the job remained dealing with... well, some of you. Customers felt entitled to raise their voices, use profanity, and commit Trumpian acts of rudeness toward my fellow employees and me. Most of our "valued guests" would never act that way in other public situations or with their own coworkers, no less friends. But inside that store, shoppers seemed to interpret "the customer is always right" to mean that they could do any damn thing they wished. It often felt as if we were penned animals who could be poked with a stick for sport, and without penalty. No matter what was said or done, store management tolerated no response from us other than a smile and a "Yes, sir" (or ma'am).

The store showed no more mercy in its treatment of workers than did the customers. My schedule, for instance, changed constantly. There was simply no way to plan things more than a week in advance. (Forget accepting a party invitation. I'm talking about childcare and medical appointments.) If you were on the closing shift, you stayed until the manager agreed that the store was clean enough for you to go home. You never quite knew when work was going to be over and no cell phone calls were allowed to alert babysitters of any delay.

And keep in mind that I was lucky. I was holding down only one job in one store. Most of my fellow workers were trying to juggle two or three jobs, each with constantly changing schedules, in order to stitch together something like a half-decent paycheck.

In New York City, that store was required to give us sick leave only after we'd worked there for a full year -- and that was generous compared to practices in many other locales. Until then, you either went to work sick or stayed home unpaid. Unlike New York, most states do not require such a store to offer any sick leave, ever, to employees who work less than 40 hours a week. Think about that the next time your waitress coughs.

MINIMUM WAGES AND MINIMUM HOURS

Much is said these days about raising the minimum wage (and it should be raised), and indeed, on January 1, 2016, 13 states did raise theirs. But what sounds like good news is unlikely to have much effect on the working poor.

In New York, for instance, the minimum went from $8.75 an hour to the $9.00 I was making. New York is relatively generous. The current federal minimum wage is $7.25 and 21 states require only that federal standard. Presumably to prove some grim point or other, Georgia and Wyoming officially mandate an even lower minimum wage and then unofficially require the payment of $7.25 to avoid Department of Labor penalties. Some Southern states set no basement figure, presumably for similar reasons.

Don't forget: any minimum wage figure mentioned is before taxes. Brackets vary, but let's knock an even 10% off that hourly wage just as a reasonable guess about what is taken out of a minimum-wage worker's salary. And there are expenses to consider, too. My round-trip bus fare every day, for instance, was $5.50. That meant I worked most of my first hour for bus fare and taxes. Keep in mind that some workers have to pay for childcare as well, which means that it's not impossible to imagine a scenario in which someone could actually come close to losing money by going to work for short shifts at minimum wage.

In addition to the fundamental problem of simply not paying people enough, there's the additional problem of not giving them enough hours to work. The two unfortunately go together, which means that raising the minimum rate is only part of any solution to improving life in the low-wage world.

At the store where I worked for minimum wage a few years ago, for instance, hours were capped at 39 a week. The company did that as a way to avoid providing the benefits that would kick in once one became a "full time" employee. Things have changed since 2012 -- and not for the better.

Four years later, the hours of most minimum-wage workers are capped at 29. That's the threshold after which most companies with 50 or more employees are required to pay into the Affordable Care Act (Obamacare) fund on behalf of their workers. Of course, some minimum wage workers get fewer than 29 hours for reasons specific to the businesses they work for.

IT'S MATH TIME

While a lot of numbers follow, remember that they all add up to a picture of how people around us are living every day.

In New York, under the old minimum wage system, $8.75 multiplied by 39 hours equaled $341.25 a week before taxes. Under the new minimum wage, $9.00 times 29 hours equals $261 a week. At a cap of 29 hours, the minimum wage would have to be raised to $11.77 just to get many workers back to the same level of take-home pay that I got in 2012, given the drop in hours due to the Affordable Care Act. Health insurance is important, but so is food.

In other words, a rise in the minimum wage is only half the battle; employees need enough hours of work to make a living.

About food: if a minimum wage worker in New York manages to work two jobs (to reach 40 hours a week) without missing any days due to illness, his or her yearly salary would be $18,720. In other words, it would fall well below the Federal Poverty Line of $21,775. That's food stamp territory. To get above the poverty line with a 40-hour week, the minimum wage would need to go above $10. At 29 hours a week, it would need to make it to $15 an hour. Right now, the highest minimum wage at a state level is in the District of Columbia at $11.50. As of now, no state is slated to go higher than that before 2018. (Some cities do set their own higher minimum wages.)

So add it up: The idea of raising the minimum wage ("the fight for $15") is great, but even with that $15 in such hours-restrictive circumstances, you can't make a loaf of bread out of a small handful of crumbs. In short, no matter how you do the math, it's nearly impossible to feed yourself, never mind a family, on the minimum wage. It's like being trapped on an M.C. Escher staircase.

The federal minimum wage hit its high point in 1968 at $8.54 in today's dollars and while this country has been a paradise in the ensuing decades for what we now call the "One Percent," it's been downhill for low-wage workers ever since. In fact, since it was last raised in 2009 at the federal level to $7.25 per hour, the minimum has lost about 8.1% of its purchasing power to inflation. In other words, minimum-wage workers actually make less now than they did in 1968, when most of them were probably kids earning pocket money and not adults feeding their own children.

In adjusted dollars, the minimum wage peaked when the Beatles were still together and the Vietnam War raged.

WHO PAYS?

Many of the arguments against raising the minimum wage focus on the possibility that doing so would put small businesses in the red. This is disingenuous indeed, since 20 mega-companies dominate the minimum-wage world. Walmart alone employs 1.4 million minimum-wage workers; Yum Brands (Taco Bell, Pizza Hut, KFC) is in second place; and McDonald's takes third. Overall, 60% of minimum-wage workers are employed by businesses not officially considered "small" by government standards, and of course carve-outs for really small businesses are possible, as was done with Obamacare.

Keep in mind that not raising wages costs you money.

Those minimum wage workers who can't make enough and need to go on food assistance? Well, Walmart isn't paying for those food stamps (now called SNAP), you are. The annual bill that states and the federal government foot for working families making poverty-level wages is $153 billion. A single Walmart Supercenter costs taxpayers between $904,542 and $1.75 million per year in public assistance money. According to Florida Congressman Alan Grayson, in many states Walmart employees are the largest group of Medicaid recipients. They are also the single biggest group of food stamp recipients. In other words, those everyday low prices at the chain are, in part, subsidized by your tax money. Meanwhile, an estimated 18% of food stamps (SNAP) are spent at Walmart.

If the minimum wage goes up, will spending on food benefits programs go down? Almost certainly. But won't stores raise prices to compensate for the extra money they will be shelling out for wages? Possibly. But don't worry -- raising the minimum wage to $15 an hour would mean a Big Mac would cost all of 17 cents more.

TIME THEFT

My retail job ended a little earlier than I had planned, because I committed time theft.

You probably don't even know what time theft is. It may sound like something from a sci-fi novel, but minimum-wage employers take time theft seriously. The basic idea is simple enough: if they're paying you, you'd better be working. While the concept is not invalid per se, the way it's used by the mega-companies reveals much about how the lowest wage workers are seen by their employers in 2016.

The problem at my chain store was that its in-store cafe was a lot closer to my work area than the time clock where I had to punch out whenever I was going on a scheduled break. One day, when break time on my shift came around, I only had 15 minutes. So I decided to walk over to that cafe, order a cup of coffee, and then head for the place where I could punch out and sit down (on a different floor at the other end of the store).

We're talking an extra minute or two, no more, but in such operations every minute is tabulated and accounted for. As it happened, a manager saw me and stepped in to tell the cafe clerk to cancel my order. Then, in front of whoever happened to be around, she accused me of committing time theft -- that is, of ordering on the clock. We're talking about the time it takes to say, "Grande, milk, no sugar, please." But no matter, and getting chastised on company time was considered part of the job, so the five minutes we stood there counted as paid work.

At $9 an hour, my per-minute pay rate was 15 cents, which meant that I had time-stolen perhaps 30 cents. I was, that is, being nickel and dimed to death.

ECONOMICS IS ABOUT PEOPLE

It seems wrong in a society as wealthy as ours that a person working full-time can't get above the poverty line. It seems no less wrong that someone who is willing to work for the lowest wage legally payable must also give up so much of his or her self-respect and dignity as a kind of tariff. Holding a job should not be a test of how to manage life as one of the working poor.

I didn't actually get fired for my time theft. Instead, I quit on the spot. Whatever the price is for my sense of self-worth, it isn't 30 cents. Unlike most of this country's working poor, I could afford to make such a decision. My life didn't depend on it. When the manager told a handful of my coworkers watching the scene to get back to work, they did. They couldn't afford not to.

1. Does the author's personal work experience change your opinion of current minimum wage laws? Why or why not?

"DIVERSE VOTERS RALLY BEHIND WAGE HIKES: ORGANIZERS SEE LOCAL AND STATE SUCCESSES IN RAISING MINIMUM WAGE," BY VINNIE ROTONDARO, FROM THE *NATIONAL CATHOLIC REPORTER*, JANUARY 2, 2015

They are white, black, Latino and Asian. They lean left and they lean right. They are rural, urban, suburban, young and old.

Almost eight years after the crash on Wall Street, with inequality soaring, what does it take to mobilize historically diverse groups of low-wage Americans, many of whom never expected to find themselves "struggling," under one economic banner?

Rocket science? Voodoo? No, minimum wage organizers say. Try basic common sense.

"The public has no trouble understanding what we are talking about," said one organizer.

It's not like we're trying to explain comprehensive immigration reform," said another.

Across America, organizers working to raise state and municipal minimum wages testify to the power of simple messaging and face-to-face appeals when reaching out to a mixed bag of voters. Focus on a straightforward, nondivisive problem, they say, get folks to rally, and move to more complex issues from there.

"Everybody wants a good job. Everybody wants to be able to work a full day and conic home and spend time with their family, or have a life outside of work," said Sara Niccoli, executive director of Labor-Religion Coalition of New York State. The coalition's Faith for a Fair New York project mobilizes faith leaders to work for economic justice.

"These are very common goals that we all share, and when we talk about them, all of a sudden, whether you're Republican or Democrat, city or country, we all basically agree."

Of course, challenges do exist. In Niccoli's case, a pronounced urban-rural divide needs bridging.

Statewide, "people view themselves as being very different despite the fact that the reality on the ground is very much the same." she said. "We always have to be thinking, 'How do we create a movement that includes both New York City its own beast, and upstate New York, which is very rural?'

"If we were just upstate," she said. "we'd be a red state."

So what works?

"Talking about poverty" she said. "Talking about wages, talking about rights at work."

In other words, the problems of a "low-wage economy" including "scheduling issues and not being able to pay the rent at the end of the month," affect people in both regions. Residents in both parts of New York get it.

"It's amazing," Niccoli said. "When we last passed a wage increase [in 2013], over 80 percent of New Yorkers supported it. Republicans, Democrats, men, women, across the age spectrum. And 80 percent of New Yorkers don't agree on anything!"

Across the country in Oakland, Calif., Jennifer Lin has seen a similar coalescence over the issue of the minimum wage.

As research director for the East Bay Alliance for a Sustainable Economy (EBASE), Lin works "mostly with people of color, low-income folks, immigrants."

This past election cycle, EBASE worked within a community, labor and faith coalition called Lift Up Oakland to introduce a ballot measure that would increase the minimum wage from $9 to $12.25 and require employers to offer sick leave.

According to a study by the University of California, Berkeley, the increase in pay and sick leave would affect about 25-30 percent of Oakland's overall workforce some 40,000 to 48,000 people--close to 80 percent of whom are either black, Latino or Asian.

Organizers knocked on doors, collected signatures, spoke with low-wage workers, attended community meetings and networked with faith leaders. On Election Day, the ballot measure passed by 82 percent.

"I think folks will say, 'Oh, it's the Bay area, of course it will pass here.' " Lin said. "But we still faced some strong opposition from the [local] chamber of commerce, which tried to do an end run around the 33,000 signatures we gathered to put our measure on the ballot."

In response, the coalition made reaching out to small businesses "a core part" of its strategy.

Meanwhile, there wasn't much difficulty getting low-wage Oakland residents on board, said Kristi Laughlin, project director for EBASE's interfaith program, Faith Alliance for a Moral Economy.

"People are suffering so much," she said, especially in the Bay area, "where the cost of living is unusually high. "No low-wage workers think what they make is adequate to live on."

According to Laughlin, crafting a ballot measure rather than seeking legislation played a crucial role in convincing voters.

Legislation would have meant working with politicians who peddled "misconceptions" about the minimum wage prior to the election, she said. Who knows how badly the result might have been carved up?

But with a ballot measure, EBASE and the Lift Up coalition were able to pinpoint what "people really need" and "not make compromises."

"And we don't see that enough," said Laughlin, a Catholic. "We're living in this national climate where you fight for what's winnable and not what's right. And there's a real power to fighting for what's right. People sense it and feel it. It's something we can all get behind."

This November, minimum wage ballot initiatives passed in four solidly conservative states--Alaska, Arkansas. Nebraska and South Dakota--as well as in two additional California cities. Additionally, nonbinding measures passed in Illinois and in nine counties and four cities in Wisconsin.

From a progressive point of view, the ballot measures were one of the only bright spots on Election Day, which saw Democrats getting trounced by Republicans and losing the Senate.

After the election, some progressives faulted the Democrat Party for not running a clearer campaign on its economic record. More generally, Democrats were accused of shying away from their core values.

Judy Conti, a practicing Catholic and the federal advocacy coordinator for the National Employment Law Project, which works "to restore the promise of economic opportunity in the 21st century economy" voices a similar criticism of some U.S. Catholic leadership in regards to the minimum wage.

"Honoring the dignity of work and workers is one of the central tenets of our faith," she said, mentioning the good work of the Jesuit Conference, the Franciscans and groups like NETWORK on the minimum wage.

Conti also brought up the June 2013 Senate testimony of Bishop Stephen Blaire of Stockton, Calif., who called it a "scandal that the richest country in the world has allowed over 23 million children in working poor families to become the norm."

Since then, the bishops of Massachusetts and Maryland issued joint statements urging state lawmakers to increase the minimum wage; additionally, in August, Bishop Edward Burns of Juneau, Alaska, wrote an opinion piece for JuneauEmpire.com supporting an increase.

As for the U.S. Conference of Catholic Bishops as a whole, Conti's feelings were mixed. The conference has not been as active on the minimum wage as it could be even, she said, despite having stated its view on the matter.

"The conference as a whole is so thoroughly devoted to the religious freedom and abortion issues, as they define them, that I think they're missing opportunities to have a meaningful impact on Capitol Hill about the things that affect the day-to-day lives of the members of their congregations who are struggling the most," she said. "I would love and welcome the opportunity for the bishops to get out there more on the minimum wage."

Conti went on to call the minimum wage a "pro-life" issue.

"One of the leading drivers for people choosing to have abortions is that they live in poverty and they know they can't afford children," she said. "You look at the Guttmacher Institute, which does the best work on tracking who has abortions and why--poverty is the single biggest driver.

"You want to stop abortions?" she said. "Raise the minimum wage. Make work pay so that people can support themselves and their families."

Similarly, many field organizers are now beginning to draw their own connections, viewing the minimum wage as a way to build bridges in society and explain more complex social justice issues.

In Nebraska, a red state where "we don't win all the time," a midterm ballot measure to raise the minimum wage passed by about 60 percent in large part because it was "so direct," said Rachel Gehringer-Wiar, field director for Nebraska Appleseed, which orchestrated a volunteer effort to collect signatures throughout the state.

"It was rare for someone not to sign the petition or to not listen to us," she said. "Even if you don't make minimum wage now, you remember when you did, or you have a friend that does, or a family member. Most people end up being connected to it in some way. It is a very straightforward thing."

Gehringer-Wiar plans on approaching the same people who signed the petition about "other issues, like Medicaid expansion." She wants to see "how far we can make those connections."

"You can't talk about the minimum wage in isolation." said Kokayi Kwa Jitahidi, campaign director of a citywide minimum wage effort for the Los Angeles Alliance for a New Economy.

"Throughout the history of social change in this country you find it's the issues that people already understand that are used as ways to build further understanding and get to deeper problems," he said.

"During the Civil Rights movement with the desegregation of lunch counters," he said, "organizers understood that it created a very clear and deeply felt experience for African-Americans." But the effort "wasn't just about desegregating lunch counters. It was always about the broader, bigger more complex issue of tearing down racial discrimination."

"The minimum wage is similar," Jitahidi explained. "Everything from workplace discrimination, to wage theft, to affordable housing--it's unique in that it touches all of these issues."

"It's a very straightforward thing," he said. "It hits on what people are experiencing."

Reprinted by permission of National Catholic Reporter, 115 E Armour Blvd, Kansas City, MO 64111 NCRonline.org

1. Ballot initiatives are often more effective that legislation, but can you foresee any potential dangers with this form of "direct democracy"?

2. Do you think raising the minimum wage is more of a symbolic "bridge" issue to address inequality, or the best possible policy lever with which to lift people out of poverty?

CONCLUSION

Many of the opinions comprised in this reader favor an increase in the minimum wage. Those arguing for this position typically downplay the negative impacts higher minimum wages may have on employment. They cite the beneficial effects of increased income and consumer spending on local economies and communities, including job growth. There is ample economic evidence to suggest this position is correct, or at least plausible enough to green light experimentation with higher minimum wages on a municipal and statewide level. Unfortunately, it is unlikely that the $15 per hour national minimum wage proposed by Bernie Sanders and others on the left will pass in the near future.

Conversely, business owners see their interests threatened if the cost of labor becomes too high. Coverage from this angle tends to feature sympathetic figures such as small shopkeepers and restaurant owners, struggling to keep their doors open amid high expenses and slim profit margins. Yet the indisputable reality is that the majority of minimum wage employees work for outrageously profitable corporations who can certainly stand to pay their workers better.

In the next few years, we can expect unionized workers to successfully secure a higher minimum wage, and also overcome the legal challenges brought on by employers. This trend has occurred notably in the state of New York, where a $15 minimum wage was signed into law by Governor Andrew Cuomo in

2016. While the threat of long-term job loss is real, it may lag behind wage increases by several years, complicating the data from these new regulations.

As it is unlikely debate over the proper level for the minimum wage will be settled anytime soon, citizens should be informed about the context, terms, and implications of these policies. We hope this reader has been of service to this end.

BIBLIOGRAPHY

Aktas, Oya. "The Intellectual History of Minimum Wage and Overtime." Washington Center for Equitable Growth, September 10, 2015. Retrieved December 18, 2015 (http://equitable-growth.org/intellectual-history-minimum-wage-overtime/).

Craighill, Peyton M. and Fletcher, Michael A. "Majority of Americans Want Minimum Wage to be Increased, Poll Finds." *The Washington Post*, December 18, 2013. Retrieved December 18, 2015 (https://www.washingtonpost.com/business/economy/majority-of-americans-want-minimum-wage-to-be-increased-poll-finds/2013/12/17/b6724bb0-6743-11e3-ae56-22de072140a2_story.html).

Griffin, Dana. "Summary of the Fair Labor Standards Act." *Chron. com.* Retrieved December 18, 2015 (http://smallbusiness.chron.com/summary-fair-labor-standards-act-2954.html).

Hall, Douglas. "Airline Industry Alert: Washington State Supreme Court Finds SeaTac Ordinance Increasing Minimum Wage To $15 An Hour Enforceable At Airport." *FordHarrison*, August 25, 2015. Retrieved November 27, 2015 (http://www.fordharrison.com/washington-state-supreme-court-finds-seatac-ordinance-increasing-minimum-wageto-15-an-hour-enforceable-at-airport).

Heriot, Gail. "Working Backwards: How Employment Regulation Hurts Unemployed Millennials."*Harvard Journal of Law & Public Policy,* Summer 2015. Retrieved November 20, 2015 (http://www.harvard-jlpp.com/wp-content/uploads/2010/01/Heriot_4.pdf).

"History of Changes to the Minimum Wage Law." US Department of Labor, 2014. Retrieved December 18, 2015 (http://www.dol.gov/whd/minwage/coverage.htm).

"House and Senate Introduces Bills to Increase Minimum Wage to $9.80." *Raise the Minimum Wage,* June 2012. Retrieved December 18, 2015 (http://www.raisetheminimumwage.com/media-center/entry/house-and-senate-intro-bills-to-increase-minimum-wage-to-9.80/).

Kramer, Will. "The Implications of Income Inequality." *Risk Management,* November 2015. Retrieved December 18, 2015 (http://www.rmmagazine.com/2015/11/02/the-implications-of-income-inequality/).

Krisberg, Kim. "Raising Minimum Wage Good for Public Health, Not Just Wallets: Advocates Call for Federal Increase." *The Nation's Health,* March 2015. November 27, 2015. Retrieved December 18, 2015 (http://thenationshealth.aphapublications.org/content/45/2/1.1.full).

Lemieux, Pierre. "From Minimum Wages to Maximum Politics: Why Is There Such a Difference of Opinion on the Employment Effects of a Minimum Wage Increase?" Regulation, 37.2 (2014). Retrieved November 17, 2015 (http://object.cato.org/sites/cato.org/files/serials/files/regulation/2014/7/regulation-v37n2-4.pdf).

Mejeur, Jeanne. "Maximum Divide on Minimum Wage: Studies Abound on the Minimum Wage, but the Conclusions Drawn Vary Greatly." *State Legislatures*, 40.3 (2014). Retrieved November 26, 2015 (http://www.ncsl.org/research/labor-and-employment/maximum-divide-on-minimum-wage.aspx).

The Minimum Wage Team (multiple authors). "The Impact of a $12 Federal Minimum Wage." *MinimumWage.com*, 2015. Retrieved December 18, 2015 (https://www.minimumwage.com/2015/11/the-impact-of-a-12-federal-minimum-wage/).

Murphy, Edward D. "Ballot Question Raising Minimum Wage to $15 Will Affect More Than Portland." *Portland Press Herald,* 18 Oct. 2015. Retrieved November 27, 2015 (http://www.pressherald.com/2015/10/18/ballot-question-raising-minimum-wage-to-15-will-impact-more-than-portland/).

Neumark, David, and William L. Wascher. *Minimum Wages.* Cambridge, MA: MIT Press, 2009.

Pacitti, Aaron. "Why Won't the Media Admit That New York's New Minimum Wage Policy Will Be Good for Business?" *Huffington Post*, August 4, 2015. Retrieved December 18, 2015 (http://www.huffingtonpost.com/aaron-pacitti/why-wont-the-media-admit-_b_7925104.html).

Reich, Robert B. "Making Work Pay: The Case for Raising the Minimum Wage." U. S. Department of Labor, March 1996. Retrieved December 18, 2015 (http://www.dol.gov/dol/about-dol/history/reich/reports/pay.htm).

Rotondaro, Vinnie. "Diverse Voters Rally Behind Wage Hikes: Organizers See Local and State Successes in Raising Minimum Wage." *National Catholic Reporter,* January 2, 2015. Retrieved December 18, 2015 (http://ncronline.org/news/politics/organizers-see-local-and-state-successes-raising-minimum-wage)

Tripp, Matt. "Why the Courts Won't Save Fast Food Companies From the $15 Minimum Wage." Eater.com, August 14, 2015. Retrieved December 18, 2015 (http://www.eater.com/2015/8/14/9149325/fight-for-15-lawsuit-minimum-wage-seattle-nyc).

Van Buren, Peter. "Nickel and Dimed in 2016: You Can't Earn a Living on the Minimum Wage." TomDispatch.com, February 16, 2016. Retrieved April 11, 2016 (http://www.tomdispatch.com/blog/176104/).

CHAPTER NOTES

CHAPTER 1: WHAT THE EXPERTS SAY

"WORKING BACKWARDS: HOW EMPLOYMENT REGULATION HURTS UNEMPLOYED MILLENNIALS," BY GAIL HERIOT

1. Elaine Sciolino and Craig S. Smith, *Protests in France Over Youth Labor Law Turn Violent*, N.Y. TIMES (Mar. 29, 2006), http://www.nytimes.com/2006/03/29/ international/europe/29france.html?pagewanted=all [http://perma.cc/4CHA-YK79].
2. *More than 1 million protest French jobs law*, CNN (Apr. 4, 2006), http://edition. cnn.com/2006/WORLD/europe/04/04/france.jobslaw/ [http://perma.cc/HJW4-ZZ7N].
3. YOUTH UNEMPLOYMENT RATE, AGED 15-24, BOTH SEXES, UN Data, http://data. un.org/Data.aspx?d=M-DG&f=seriesRowID%3A630 [http://perma.cc/WSY3-DUDK].
4. *See Fresh job law protests in France,* BBC NEWS (Apr. 4, 2006), http://news.bbc. co.uk/2/hi/europe/4874414.stm [http://perma. cc/WC3U-TS36].
5. *See* Richard Epstein, *Contractual Solutions for Employment Law Problems*, 38 HARV. J.L. & PUB. POL'Y 787 (2015); *but see* J.H. Verkerke, *Employment Regulation and Youth Employment: A Critical Perspective,* 38 HARV. J.L. & PUB. POL'Y 801 (2015).
6. *See France to replace youth job law,* BBC NEWS (Apr. 10, 2006), http://news.bbc. co.uk/2/hi/europe/4895164.stm [http://perma. cc/7RQT-R6J7].
7. Labor Force Statistics from the Current Population Survey, BUREAU OF LABOR STATISTICS, *available* at http://www.bls.gov/web/empsit/cpseea10.htm [http:// perma.cc/2B-ZP-T6A5] (showing youth unemployment rate, and unemployment rates for ages 35-44 years, 45-54 years, and 55 years and over at 4.4%, 4.1%, and 3.9%, respectively).
8. *See* Danielle Paquette, *The early results from America's experiments with higher minimum wages,* WASH. POST (Aug. 4, 2014), http://www.washingtonpost.com/ news/storyline/wp/2014/08/04/the-early-results-from-americas-experiments-withhigher-minimum-wages/ [http://perma.cc/8YMG-3Z7Y] (showing numbers in Seattle); John Coté, *Higher minimum wage wins with big support in SF and Oakland*, SFGATE (Nov. 4, 2014), http://www.sfgate.com/bayarea/article/High-

er-minimumwage-in-SF-leading-easily-in-early- 5871304.php [http://perma.cc/RQ6E-HGYU].

9. *See Why some economists oppose minimum wages*, ECONOMIST, Jan. 22, 2014, http://www.economist.eom/blogs/economist-ex-plains/2014/01/economist- explains11?zid=309&ah=80d-cf288b8561b012f603b9fd9577f0e [http://perma.cc/PG3L-HS4W].

10. David Card & Alan B. Krueger, *Minimum Wages and Employ-ment: A Case Study of the Fast-Food Industry in New Jersey and Pennsylvania*, 84 AM. ECON. REV. 772, 773 (1994).

11. Alex Konrad, *Applebee's Will Install 100,000 Intel-Backed Tablets Next Year In Record Rollout*, FORBES (Dec. 3, 2013), http://www.forbes.com/sites/alexkonrad/ 2013/12/03/applebees-intel-tab-let-rollout/ [http://perma.cc/7X46-UC5M].

12. Steve Rosen, *Applebee's plans to bring tablet computers to every table next year*, KANSAS CITY STAR (Dec. 3, 2013), http://www.kansascity.com/news/local/ article333068/Applebee's-plans-to-bring-tablet-computers-to-every-table-nextvear.html [http://perma.ee/HT36-5UFD] (stating that the restaurant chain "will install 100,000 tablet computers in its more than 1,800 locations nationwide by the end of next year"); *see also* Sean William, *Why Applebee's Tablets May Need a Reboot*, MOTLEY FOOL (Aug. 16, 2014) http://www.fool.com/investing/gen-eral/2014/08/16/ why-applebees-tablets-may-need-a-reboot.aspx [http://perma.cc/G3TY-VZXP] (stating that Applebee's plans to finish installing tablets in 2015 and "expects to be near halfway complete with the rollout by year's end").

13. *See* Card & Krueger, *supra* note 10, at 772 (showing increase from $4.25 to $5.05 per hour).

14. ROSS PERLIN, INTERN NATION: HOW TO EARN NOTH-ING AND LEARN LITTLE IN THE BRAVE NEW ECONOMY 203 (2011).

15. *Id*. at 223.

16. *See* 42 U.S.C. [section] 2000e-2 (2012) (rule on failing to hire or discharging employees).

17. *Id*. [section] 2000e(b) (definition of employer).

18. *See* STATE LAWS ON EMPLOYMENT RELATED DIS-CRIMINATION, NATIONAL CONFERENCE OF STATE LEGISLATURES, http://www.ncsl.org/research/labor-andem-ployment/discrimination-employment.aspx [http://perma.cc/V365-PNM6] (showing some states, such as Arkansas, Alaska, Georgia, and others that have discrimination laws that apply to employers with fewer than fifteen employees).

19. *See* 42 U.S.C. [section] 2000e-5(g)(2)(B)(i) (2012).
20. *See* Christiansburg Garment Co. v. Equal Emp't Opportunity Comm'n, 434 U.S. 412, 420-22 (1978).
21. 401 U.S. 424 (1971).
22. Id. at 429-30.
23. *See* Ricci v. DeStefano, 557 U.S. 557, 594-96 (2009) (Scalia, J., concurring).
24. *See, e.g.,* Harry J. Holzer et at, *Perceived Criminality, Criminal Background Checks, and the Racial Hiring Practices of Employers,* *49* J.L. & ECON. 451, 451 (2006) (finding that "employers who check criminal backgrounds are more likely to hire African American workers, especially men," thus suggesting that "some employers discriminate statistically against black men and/or those with weak employment records").

CHAPTER 4: ADVOCACY GROUPS FOR AND AGAINST THE MINIMUM WAGE INCREASE

"THE INTELLECTUAL HISTORY OF MINIMUM WAGE AND OVERTIME," BY OYA AKTAS

1. Edward James McKenna and Diane Catherine Zannoni, "Economics and the Supreme Court: The Case of the Minimum Wage," *Review of Social Economy* 69 (2) (2011): 189-209.
2. Arthur N. Holcombe, "The Legal Minimum Wage in the United States," *The American Economic Review* 2 (1) (1912): 21-37.
3. "Police Power: American Law," available at www.britannica.com/topic/police-power (last accessed August 2015).
4. "Muller v. Oregon," available at www.law.cornell.edu/ supreme-court/text/208/412 (last accessed August 2015).
5. Robert E. Prasch "American Economists in the Progressive Era on the Minimum Wage," *Journal of Economic Perspectives* 13 (2) (1999): 221-230.
6. Arthur N. Holcombe, "The Effects of the Legal Minimum Wage for Women," *Annals of the American Academy of Political and Social Science 69* (1917): 34-41.
7. Marilyn Power, "Parasitic-Industries Analysis and Arguments for a Living Wage for Women in the Early Twentith-Century United States," *Feminist Economics* 5 (1) (1999): 61-78.

8. Ellen Mutari, Marilyn Power, and Deborah M. Figart, "Neither Mothers Nor Breadwinners," *Feminist Economics* 8 (2) (2002): 37-61.

9. Arthur N. Holcombe, "The Legal Minimum Wage in the United States," *The American Economic Review* 2 (1) (1912): 21-37.

10. "Adkins v. Children's Hospital (1923)," available at www.pbs.org/wnet/supremecourt/capitalism/landmark_adkins.html (last accessed August 2015).

11. Edward James McKenna and Diane Catherine Zannoni, "Economics and the Supreme Court: The Case of the Minimum Wage," *Review of Social Economy* 69 (2) (2011). 189-209.

12. Kristin Downey, *The Woman Behind the New Deal* (New York: Anchor Books, 2009).

13. "Birth of the Minimum Wage in America," www.npr.org/sections/money/2014/01/16/263129670/the-birth-of-theminimum-wage-in-america (last available August 2015).

14. "West Coast Hotel Co. v. Parrish," available at www.oyez.org/cases/1901-1939/1936/1936 293 (last accessed August 2015).

15. Kristin Downey, *The Woman Behind the New Deal* (New York: Anchor Books, 2009).

16. Ira Katznelson, *Fear Itself,* (New York: Liveright Publishing Corporation, 2013).

17. "The Benefits of Increasing the Minimum Wage for People of Color," available at www.americanprogress.org/issues/race/news/2014/04/21/87248/the-benefits-of-increasingthe-minimum-wage-for-people-of-color/ (last accessed August 2015); "By the Numbers: A Look at the Gender Pay Gap," available at http://www.aauw.org/2014/09/18/ gender-pay-gap/ (last accessed August 2015).

GLOSSARY

average hourly rate—A figure obtained by dividing total wages by hours worked.

base rate—The level of pay prior to tips, commissions, or other incentive-based forms of compensation.

benefits—Extra-wage compensation including retirement, insurance, paid leave, supplementary pay, and other legally-required social assistance.

collective bargaining—The process by which unions and employers negotiate agreements regarding work conditions and compensation. Agreements are usually applicable for a limited timeframe.

consumer price index—A monthly figure published by the Bureau of Labor Statistics measuring average changes in price for goods and services.

cost of living adjustment—Built-in wage or salary increases to compensate for higher prices and housing costs. These are determined by the Consumer Price Index.

entrance rate—The rate of pay at which a new employee begins work.

Fair Labor Standards Act of 1938 (FLSA)—A federal law designed to reduce exploitation and child labor, a crucial part of which was to introduce overtime pay and a minimum wage.

living wage—A wage that not only covers the basic expenses of life, but also allows a modicum of savings and discretionary spending.

minimum wage—The lowest legal rate of pay an employer can pay an employee. The minimum wage varies from state to state. Some exceptions to the minimum wage apply, such as internships and training wages.

overtime pay—A rate of pay that is usually equivalent to 1.5 times the normal wage a worker receives. Employers are mandated to pay this rate for hours exceeding forty per week.

parental leave—Parental leave is sanctioned work leave for a new parent to care for his or her child, which can be paid or unpaid.

pay compression—Reduction of pay inequality across workers in a firm or industry.

real wages—A measure of the buying power of wages accounting for price changes.

union—An organization that engages in bargaining and other essential activities on behalf of a group of workers.

wage rate—The amount per hour a worker receives for doing his or her job.

ABOUT THE EDITOR

Anne Cunningham has a PhD in Comparative Literature, and has published articles on women modernist writers and feminist theory. She currently works as an Instructor of English at the University of New Mexico—Taos. She is also a songwriter and performer, and lives with her husband and music partner David Lerner in Arroyo Hondo, NM.

FOR MORE INFORMATION

BOOKS

Abramsky, Sasha. *The American Way of Poverty: How the Other Half Still Lives*. New York: Nation Books, 2014

Berlatsky, Noah. *The Minimum Wage (Opposing Viewpoints)*. Boston: Cengage, 2012

Ehrenreich, Barbara. *Nickel and Dimed: On (Not) Getting by in America*. New York: Holt Paperbacks, 2011.

Katz, Michael. *The Undeserving Poor: America's Enduring Confrontation with Poverty*. Oxford: Oxford UP, 2013.

Piketty, Thomas. *Capital in the Twenty-First Century*. Cambridge: Harvard University Press, 2014.

Piketty, Thomas. *The Economics of Inequality*. Cambridge: Harvard University Press, 2015.

Reich, Robert. *Saving Capitalism: For the Many, Not the Few*. Toronto: Knopf, 2015.

Royce, Edward. *Poverty and Power: The Problem of Structural Inequality*. New York: Rowman & Littlefield, 2015.

Stiglitz, Joseph. *The Price of Inequality: How Today's Divided Society Endangers Our Future*. New York: WW Norton & Co., 2013.

Tirado, Linda. *Hand to Mouth: Living in Bootstrap America*. Berkeley: Berkley Press, 2015.

WEBSITES

United States Department of Labor: Wage and Hour Division
www.dol.gov/whd/minimumwage.htm

This site, administered by the United States Department of
Labor, is one of the best resources available online for all
things minimum wage. It is neutral and multilingual, and
contains a comprehensive overview of FLSA (Federal Labor
Standards Act) laws and updates. It also has scholarly articles
on the history of workplace laws and regulations.

Raise the Minimum Wage
www.raisetheminimumwage.com

Raise the Minimum Wage is a site lobbying for increased
minimum wages. The site presents information related to
this nationwide struggle, with a focus on advocacy groups
such as "Fight for $15." Started in conjunction with the
National Employment Law Project, the site is presently the
best resource for up-to-date information about efforts to raise
the minimum wage, and how to support or partner with such
efforts locally and nationwide.

Minimum Wage
www.minimumwage.com

Another partisan site, minimumwage.com is administered by
the non-profit Employment Policies Institute (EPI), and is
opposed to policies aimed at increasing the minimum wage.
Arguments debunking the supposed economic benefits of
higher minimum wages are collected under the site's "Myths"
heading. In addition, state-by-state information, research, and
blog posts can be found on the site.

INDEX